NEW NOISE

Steve Jones
General Editor

Vol. 88

The Digital Formations series is part of the Peter Lang Media and Communication list.
Every volume is peer reviewed and meets
the highest quality standards for content and production.

PETER LANG
New York • Washington, D.C./Baltimore • Bern
Frankfurt • Berlin • Brussels • Vienna • Oxford

Simon Lindgren

NEW NOISE

A Cultural Sociology
of Digital Disruption

PETER LANG
New York • Washington, D.C./Baltimore • Bern
Frankfurt • Berlin • Brussels • Vienna • Oxford

Library of Congress Cataloging-in-Publication Data
Lindgren, Simon.
New noise: a cultural sociology of digital disruption / Simon Lindgren.
p. cm. — (Digital formations; vol. 88)
Includes bibliographical references and index.
1. Digital media. 2. Social networks. 3. Digital divide. I. Title.
HM851.L552   302.23'1—dc23   2012039909
ISBN 978-1-4331-1995-8 (hardcover)
ISBN 978-1-4331-1994-1 (paperback)
ISBN 978-1-4539-0948-5 (e-book)
ISSN 1526-3169

Bibliographic information published by **Die Deutsche Nationalbibliothek**
Die Deutsche Nationalbibliothek lists this publication in the "Deutsche
Nationalbibliografie"; detailed bibliographic data is available
on the Internet at http://dnb.d-nb.de/.

The paper in this book meets the guidelines for permanence and durability
of the Committee on Production Guidelines for Book Longevity
of the Council of Library Resources.

CONTENTS

Acknowledgments   vii
Foreword   ix

Chapter 1. The Double Trap   1
Chapter 2. In Search of Space   19
Chapter 3. Shapes, Relations, Structures   37
Chapter 4. Hacktivist Mobilization   49
Chapter 5. Network Politics   65
Chapter 6. *.Sub Culture   79
Chapter 7. Holy Shit! It Works!!   93
Chapter 8. Plural Reactions   111
Chapter 9. The Subactivist Challenge   125
Chapter 10. A Cultural Sociology of Digital Disruption   139

Works Cited   151
Index   161

ACKNOWLEDGMENTS

Some of the empirical work presented in this book has also been reported elsewhere. Chapter 4 is based on an article published in *New Media and Society* (Lindgren & Lundström, 2011), and chapter 7 has been published in a slightly different form in the *European Journal of Communication* (Lindgren, 2012). Chapter 8 builds on a text that was included in *Media, Culture and Society* (Lindgren, 2011), and chapter 9 draws heavily on a piece from *Convergence* (Lindgren & Linde, 2012). I would like to thank my co-authors Jessica Linde and Ragnar Lundström for their valuable contributions. The writing of this book has been partly funded by the Swedish Research Council (through the project *Filesharing and Sense of Justice*), the Knowledge Foundation (through the program *YouTube as a Performative Arena*), and the Swedish Council for Working Life and Social Research (through the project *Social Media and Political Participation*).

FOREWORD
by David Gauntlett

A few pages into *New Noise*, Simon Lindgren provides a telling quote from John Fiske's book *Understanding Popular Culture*. Fiske observes, with dismay, that scholars of popular culture have typically fallen into one of two camps: those who don't situate their analysis within 'a model of power', and so are free to be nice about their subject matter, and those who do, and therefore feel obliged to condemn it. Both approaches therefore become predictable rather than challenging. Fiske suggests that there could be a 'third direction', which balances consideration of the power of media systems with the power of ordinary people. What a novel idea!

Fiske's book was published in 1989, almost 25 years ago. For me, this was the year I left home and went to university. The media landscape in the UK was print, radio, and 4 channels of TV; the World Wide Web had not been invented yet. 'Interactivity' referred to the capacity to call up a weather forecast on teletext, which, as the name suggested, was a set of texts available on your telly. In short, it was *ages* ago.

Since then, the idea of a 'third way' in other spheres—notably politics—has come to seem ordinary, and then outdated. It is ordinary because it's no longer a new idea, but also because the general principle came to be broadly accepted, even if the 'third way' phrase was not. In many countries, mainstream politics is rarely about genuinely left-wing versus right-wing ideas these days, and the middle-ground third way describes the standard arena for a majority of political parties (although the 'third way' was really meant to be a radical *alternative* to the norm, not just a middle-of-the-road view).

In media and communications studies, however, Fiske's argument could be presented tomorrow and would still seem fresh and relevant. The technologies and opportunities have changed to a huge extent, but the approaches of media scholars have not. Indeed, if it seemed for a while—during, say, the first decade of the 21st century—that the old boundaries had shifted, we now see the lines being redrawn more sharply. Scholars such as Christian Fuchs (2008, 2011) have led a thoughtful but decidedly Marxist restatement of what's wrong with today's media system. James Curran, Natalie Fenton and Des Freedman received warm reviews for *Misunderstanding the Internet* (2012), a book which lives up to its title by mixing a less sophisticated kind of Marxism with a surprising nostalgia for a time when only elites could express themselves in widely-available media. Meanwhile, incisive but less partisan analysts, such as Clay Shirky (2008, 2010), who take an interest in what social media might mean within the lives of their users, are dismissed as 'evangelists' for new technologies merely because they have failed to join in with a more knee-jerk rejection of their possible value.

So, a 'third way' in media and communications studies would be very welcome. And that is what Lindgren offers in this timely and persuasive book.

I have known Simon Lindgren for a few years. I say 'known,' but until recently we had not met in person. As noted above, things changed a lot over the past quarter century, so like many modern relationships, this one began online. But really, when I finally met him on a visit to London, it didn't make that much difference. He was as I had known him via electronic communication: modest, intelligent, generous.

I was pleased to be invited to write a foreword for his new book, which I understood to be called *New Noise*. I expected it would be good but didn't know what it would be about. So I was even happier when I received the manuscript with the subtitle, A *Cultural Sociology of Digital Disruption*. The notion of 'disruptions' has been central to my thinking about new technologies, in particular anything running on the internet, for a while now. I like it for the straightforward visual image which it suggests of something erupting from below and breaking apart what was already there. And I mean: *in a good way*. To illustrate the idea of disruptions in a presentation, I tend to use Google image search to grab pictures of dramatic earthquakes which have smashed up some important bit of infrastructure. Of course, those are not happy events. But the disruptions in media and communications which the internet has made possible are almost always exciting and interesting innovations, even if their outcomes are not universally desirable.

The digital disruptions or transformations which potentially affect scholars of media and communications can be divided into three spheres:

- Disruptions or transformations in our objects of study—communications systems, materials and services themselves
- Disruptions or transformations in how we study them—new methods and approaches
- Disruptions or transformations in how we communicate and have conversations about these phenomena and this research

So it's about *what* we study, *how* we study it, and how we *engage* others about it. Only the first of these describes the task of keeping up with one's subject matter, which is an established, predictable thing that you have to do as a scholar of any subject. The other two potentially undermine and screw up the established way of doing things, and are therefore especially exciting. In any case, Lindgren covers all three: the first, in his substantial analysis of a changing media landscape and what people do in it; the second, with his innovative data-mining methodology, Connected Concept Analysis, which offers 'a qualitative approach to quantity' (see Chapter 3); and third—although perhaps to a lesser extent in this traditional object, a book—in his online videos, blog and tweets.

In *New Noise*, Lindgren steers a path between what technical systems can do within a culture, and how people within that culture respond and innovate for themselves. Of course, that means it's not just a study of how humans respond to their technological environment, because those technical systems were themselves responses and innovations, made by humans, to previously existing aspects of technology and culture. It is therefore, in the old-fashioned terminology of media studies, about integrating the study of 'media institutions' and 'media technologies' with the study of 'media audiences' or 'media users'. This is the kind of 'third way' that media scholars have been calling for

for a long time. But more significantly, it cleverly mirrors the concept of structuration as developed by Anthony Giddens (1984), who was also the preeminent advocate of the 'third way' in social theory and politics (Giddens, 1998).

The theory of structuration was Giddens' attempt to overcome the unhelpful divide between those who studied societies or cultures on a macro level (for example, in our case, what media institutions and systems do) and those who focused on the micro level (here, what media users do). He achieved this by noting the cycle of influence between the two levels: the macro level defines the circumstances within which people operate, but then people's actions can, cumulatively and over time, bring about changes in the collective understanding of a culture, which gradually changes the macro level itself; which changes what people within that culture consider to be possible or legitimate; and so on. Simon Lindgren offers something similar here, showing how the normally separate spheres of media systems and media users are connected in a mutually dependent cycle.

It's never straightforward or simple, though. Across a series of case studies, Lindgren observes how collaboration and conflict go hand-in-hand, and that online communication and creativity is always a complex criss-crossing of different kinds of inputs, done for many diverse reasons, with an array of simultaneous, contradictory outcomes which are never the final word on a situation but merely the starting point for further complex interactions. Multiplied by several million.

This is all a bit too vast to be thinkable, so the case studies help to bring focus. In the case of YouTube, for example (Chapter 7), Lindgren finds that those who leave comments can be casually antagonistic when they are acting as individual consumers/participants. The lack of a shared sense of a project often leaves them with just a 'thumbs up' or 'thumbs down' response to the work of others. But when people felt that they were collectively engaged in something together—as Lindgren finds in the comments attached to user-created tutorial videos, where people *want* to share their learning with others who are *seeking* that input—the comments are much more positive and oriented to helping others, even where those others are geographically remote, and invisible, and you're unlikely to ever meet any of them.

In other words, it is the *binding* of people into a shared enterprise which makes all the difference. This is what I argued in *Making is Connecting* (2011), but it's nice to see it supported with new empirical examples and with Lindgren's thoughtful insights. Similarly, the study of those who create and share subtitles files for movies and TV series (Chapter 6) shows that a common project leads people to be aggressively altruistic, but also altruistically aggressive: Lindgren quotes examples of users who are so passionately engaged in the project of making high-quality subtitles available that they get just as passionately cross when other people are not contributing in what they see as the 'correct' way.

These observations are at the 'micro' end, on the quality of social interactions. Lindgren's concerns are also, of course, political, and these interests play out in both macro and micro settings. In particular he has a concern with 'spaces', which I think you can picture like pockets of conversation being temporarily inflated, by groups of people, in the zone between the crowded micro level of individuals on the ground and the more abstract macro level of society, culture, and economic and communications systems, above. While academic talk about 'space' and 'spaces' is often maddeningly abstract, in Chapter 4 Lindgren manages to show how a Twitter hashtag—barely a 'thing' at all—can function as a 'virtual settlement', which pops up in a more-or-less unplanned way and becomes the site of discussions, *through* usage, for as long as people want it. These conversations, whilst apparently non-organised and open and therefore quite 'anarchic', also tend to follow certain rules and norms; Lindgren shows, in effect, that human beings are quite good at participating in communities even when nobody has set any formal laws, or restrictions, or told us what to do.

The earlier observation that nothing is straightforward or simple—in the relationship between macro level cultures and micro level behaviours—is especially brought to life in the interviews with online movie pirates in Chapter 9. Here we find individuals who see themselves as political actors, who are repelled by the commercial system of Hollywood movies, and who express this by sharing and viewing illegal copies of those movies. There seemed to me to be a weird contradiction here—fighting the hated Hollywood culture by means of consuming its products. I'm keen on people using the internet for creative and innovative purposes, and I'm keen to see the circulation of alternatives to mainstream art and entertainment. But sharing and watching copies of commercial movies that you, apparently, don't even like, doesn't seem to fulfil any of these aspirations, so I found it a bit odd. What it *does* show is that the flows of creativity and resistance between the macro and micro levels of a culture can be sometimes powerful, sometimes quirky and confused, and never entirely predictable.

Throughout this book, Lindgren looks at forms of cultural disruption which have political implications, or which relate to politics, but which are also subtle and complex, and don't always point in one clear direction. Readers looking for evidence that technology 'X' produced revolutionary change 'Y' are likely to be disappointed. But we should applaud the author for his insistence that theories about the relationships between technologies and culture should be based on 'what actually happens'. To the external observer this may sound strangely obvious, but claims-making in this sphere is often based on ideology rather than a good understanding of how things work and what is really going on. As Lindgren says in the concluding chapter, 'Ultimately this book is a plea for taking internet studies into a new era of systematic empirical inquiry of the processes by which the power of the good examples might be harnessed towards a more substantial transformation of the public'.

Lindgren avoids simplistic binaries, refusing to find that certain technologies are 'good' or 'bad', or politically 'effective' or 'ineffective'. Instead, he offers insights into the complexities of the ways in which technologies are used, whilst also offering hope—'the power of the good examples'—that we can foster and harness creative and disruptive practices, whether in learning, community-building, entertainment, politics, self-expression, or other spheres. He reminds us that complex networks of differently-motivated activities can still offer challenges to the status quo, and the 'new noise' might be a cacophony of voices asking how we can do things in better, fairer, and more inspiring ways.

—David Gauntlett
August 2012

References

Curran, James P. Fenton, Natalie, & Freedman, Des (2012), *Misunderstanding the Internet*. London: Routledge.

Fuchs, Christian (2008), *Internet and Society: Social Theory in the Information Age*. London: Routledge.

Fuchs, Christian (2011), *Foundations of Critical Media and Information Studies*. London: Routledge.

Gauntlett, David (2011), *Making Is Connecting: The Social Meaning of Creativity, from DIY and Knitting to YouTube and Web 2.0*. Cambridge, UK: Polity.

Giddens, Anthony (1984), *The Constitution of Society: Outline of the Theory of Structuration*. Cambridge, UK: Polity.

Giddens, Anthony (1998), *The Third Way: The Renewal of Social Democracy*. Cambridge, UK: Polity.

Shirky, Clay (2008), *Here Comes Everybody: The Power of Organising Without Organisations*. London: Allen Lane.

Shirky, Clay (2010), *Cognitive Surplus: Creativity and Generosity in a Connected Age*. London: Allen Lane.

· 1 ·

THE DOUBLE TRAP

The information society is a trap. (Lévy, 1999, p. 31)

From Tahrir Square to Wall Street, in remix culture and fan fiction, in social media election campaigns and digitally coordinated flashmobs, in Internet piracy and culture jamming, today, an increasing number of digital sociocultural spaces are celebrated for being disruptive. Currents stemming from these spaces allegedly have the power to circumvent dominant flows of communication, to subvert preferred meanings, and to challenge the powers that be. Claims about the character and significance of this power are at the center of an ongoing debate over the effects of digital culture on the nature of hegemony and resistance in the spheres of economy, politics, and culture. Beyond the hype lies immense polarization. Cultural commentators provide us with alternating images of "slacktivism" on the one hand, and of "Twitter revolutions" on the other. Scholarly writers, similarly, fall into two camps: allegedly naïve optimists and their counterparts, skeptical critics. This book, however, takes its cue from Lovink's (2002, p.11) idea of the existence of a radical pragmatism that moves "[b]eyond resignation and the romance of revolt." "[N]o more vapor theory anymore," he writes; "Enough techno-mysticism and digital Darwinism. Neither do we need techno-cultural pessimism" (2002, p. 10).

What we need are actual studies, not philosophical poses. Indeed, most digital media strategies—whether they are enacted by businesspeople or activists—are "living paradoxes rooted in a messy praxis" (Lovink, 2002, p. 226). We live in an increasingly complex world, and this book tries to advance and reload a cultural sociology for the study of this messiness. Radical pragmatism "requires vigilant efforts to articulate the net with materiality, for herein lies the possibility of a politics that recognizes the embeddedness of social practices" (Lovink, 2002, p. 13). This articulation must be done by activists and academics alike, and this book aims to make a contribution by specifically focusing on digital (disruptive) space situated at the nexus of possibility and praxis.

Examples such as the ones mentioned—ranging from uprisings and occupations to struggles over signification and intellectual property—are unified by the circumstance that in their current forms, they all have a strong relation to digital culture. Furthermore, they all represent efforts to interfere with dominant regimes of representation, politics, and economy. They do this in a wide variety of settings, and with different motivations. This book is not about digital politics or hacktivism in any specific form. Nor is it about fan culture, pirate culture, remix culture, or virtual community. At the same time, it is about all of the above. It is an exploration of the type of emergent online spaces that may function as a springboard for movements in all of these fields. Throughout this book, I call them *disruptive spaces*. The use of this term should not be interpreted as an assumption that there are spaces in digital culture that are disruptive in essence and by nature. Nor should it be taken to mean that all attempts at disruption using digital tools and platforms automatically succeed (or fail). I suggest the concept as the starting point for a cultural sociology aiming to identify potentially, or self-proclaimed, disruptive spaces in order to assess whether they are, actually, spaces, and if they are, in fact, disruptive.

Some writers are quite optimistic about the revolutionary potential of digital media, arguing that the lowered thresholds for participation and user production will contribute to a significant transformation of culture and society (Rheingold, 2002; Jenkins, 2006; Shirky, 2008). Others are more skeptical, claiming that even though the Internet provides a global and largely decentralized communication infrastructure, the notion of participatory digital culture also has ideological dimensions, and that capitalist processes of hegemony and exploitation are still at large, making counter-power difficult to deploy (Fuchs, 2011; Morozov, 2011). Galloway (2004, pp. 245–246) suggests that the digital development in many ways "is a dramatic move forward, but in other ways it reinstates systems of social and technical control that are deserving of critical analysis."

This book takes its starting point in "the broadening of the political, where all social realities become, at least potentially, contestable and politicized" (Carpentier, 2011, p. 40). The gradual emergence in late modern societies of a diversity of political practices, originating from actors positioned outside of institutionalized politics, has widened the scope of the political. Carpentier (2011, p. 39) states that "we witness [not only] a broadening of the set of actors involved in political activities, but also an expansion of the spheres that are considered political." The case studies throughout this book include digital piracy, social media mobilization, knowledge communities, fan communities, and YouTube discussion threads. While vastly different in several ways, they are all happening in relation to potentially disruptive spaces that are political in the sense that they challenge dominant ways of doing politics, culture, and learning. As we shall see, they all relate to "the political" as defined by Mouffe (2000, p. 101):

> By "the political," I refer to the dimension of antagonism that is inherent in human relations, antagonism that can take many forms and emerge in different types of social relations.

At best, the disruptive spaces represent new noise—emergent cultural currents that are part of a dramatic transformation of the social and cultural fabric, and that enable unprecedented forms of potent rebellion within a number of areas. At worst, they are idealized techno-deterministic fantasies blinded by utopian promises of networked media and failing to account for the continued power of capitalism. In this book, I set out to discover, map, and theorize this terrain. It is about contextualizing what happens in potentially disruptive spaces, and about critically discussing the ability of these cells to connect with each other to provide a substantial challenge to prevailing orders. Can the millions of niches and enclaves of "long tail" culture (Anderson, 2006) be added up to a functioning counterpublic (Habermas, 1989; Warner, 2002b), or is the fragmentation definitive?

Important debates about downsides to Web 2.0 and participatory culture are often undermined by the black-or-white stereotyping and distortions of arguments that run in both directions between unreflected techno-optimists (cf. Fuchs, 2011, p. 290) and technophobic cultural pessimists (cf. Lovink, Rossiter et al., 2009). Such polarizations help to obscure the fact that alleged pessimists and supposed optimists often share the view that there is a strong transformatory and progressive potential in digital culture, but that we must not assume that this potential is realized automatically and without friction and inequalities.

The debate is further compromised by the different focuses among these different interpretations and strategies. As Gauntlett (2011) shows, many digital platforms may indeed be profitable businesses. YouTube, for example, can make large advertising revenues off the creative, free work of their users. But we must not assume that this obvious exploitation is viewed as such by the individual user. Although audiences may be exploited at the structural level, this does not exclude the possibility that they get something rewarding for themselves from their work, or that their efforts may generate results apart from advertising money for big business. In the end, the degree of realization of the positive potentialities is not a philosophical question, but an empirical one. The most productive position for the researcher seems to be one that manages to balance the "critical" and "celebratory" positions, taking into account structure as well as agency. A parallel to this argument is found in what Fiske wrote about the analysis of popular culture in the 1980s:

> Until recently, the study of popular culture has taken two main directions. The less productive has been that which has celebrated popular culture without situating it in a model of power [. . . .] The other direction has been to situate popular culture firmly within a model of power, but to emphasise so strongly the forces of domination as to make it appear impossible for a genuine popular culture to exist at all [. . . .] Recently, however, a third direction has begun to emerge [. . . .] It, too, sees popular culture as a site of struggle, but, while accepting the power of the forces of dominance, it focuses rather upon the popular tactics by which these forces are coped with, are evaded or are resisted. (Fiske, 1989, p. 19)

I will attempt, with this book, to take the study of digital culture and participation in this third direction by focusing on the intersection of structure and agency at the site of particular spaces—because there are obviously some sort of disruptive spaces with some sort of effect. I ask in this book: What, precisely, are these spaces? What do they do? And to what specific contextualized effects? What characterizes the disruptive spaces, and how might they be understood in relation to the wider framework of hegemony and resistance, publics and counterpublics? It comes down to evaluating, in relation to various types of empirical data, whether, how, to what degree, and under which circumstances digital media are part of a realization of emancipatory projects. How are successful tactics enacted, and what kind of leverage do they have in the face of capitalist, governmental, hegemonic powers? The following sections move through a set of theoretical foundations for the analyses and discussions that follow in this book.

Beyond Technophilia and Technophobia

[T]he development of interactive, horizontal networks of communication has induced the rise of a new form of communication, mass self-communication, over the Internet and wireless communication networks. Under these conditions, insurgent politics and social movements are able to intervene more decisively in the new communication space. However, corporate media and mainstream politics have also invested in this new communication space. (Castells, 2007, p. 238)

Moving in a radical pragmatist direction in order to evade "the double trap of blind technophilia and luddite technophobia" (Lovink, Rossiter et al. 2009, p. 10) does not mean rejecting all previously suggested concepts in digital studies. I will use theoretical notions stemming from both sides of the cyberculture divide as stepping stones for developing a contextualized understanding of disruptive spaces. In fact, all the themes I deal with boil down to the division between repressive and emancipatory uses of media as described by Enzensberger (1970). In this forty-year-old essay on "new electronic media" he manages to condense much of the rhetoric and academic discourse surrounding digital culture today. First, he notes that new media have become "the pacemaker for the social and economic development of societies in the late industrial age" (p. 13). All the new forms of emerging media that he identifies—"news satellites, colour television, cable relay television, cassettes, videotape, videotape recorders, video-phones, stereophony, laser techniques, electrostatic reproduction processes, electronic high-speed printing, composing and learning machines, microfiches with electronic access, printing by radio, time-sharing computers, data banks"—are, he claims, constantly making new connections with each other as well as with older media. Preceding the more recent theorizations of media convergence (Jenkins, 2006), Enzensberger writes that all media "are clearly coming together to form a universal system" (1970, p. 14).

Enzensberger expressed an optimistic view of the new electronic media and distanced himself from what he felt were nonproductive media criticisms of the socialist left. For this he was criticized by, amongst others, Baudrillard (1981, p. 168), who argued that although Enzensberger "attempts to develop an optimistic and offensive position [...] [t]he media are monopolized by the dominant classes, which divert them to their own advantage." Enzensberger's argument is that the media are fundamentally egalitarian, and that it is up to media users to realize their potential.

Baudrillard (1981, p. 168) agreed that the media are liberatory, "but it is necessary to liberate them." He goes on to say that "[t]he mass media are anti-mediatory and intransitive. They fabricate non-communication—this is what characterizes them" (p. 169). Kellner (1996, p. 2), on the other hand, dismisses Baudrillard's argument as an expression of "technophobia and a nostalgia for face-to-face conversation." Once again, then, we are caught in the by now familiar deadlock: New electronic/digital media surely have a liberatory potential, but one can be either optimistic or skeptical as regards its disengagement. Still, Enzensberger's (1970, p. 26) typology summarizes the debate rather well. His schematic thematization is illustrated in Table 1.

The following sections will be devoted to a summary of perspectives that can be read in terms of Enzensberger's typology. We will look first at various conceptualizations of emancipatory media use in the form of two potentialities: the development and interconnection of fluid skill zones, and participa-

Table 1: Enzensberger's Typology of Emancipatory and Repressive Use of Media

Emancipatory use of media	Repressive use of media
Decentralized programme	Centrally controlled programme
Each receiver a potential transmitter	One transmitter, many receivers
Mobilization of the masses	Immobilization of isolated individuals
Interaction of those involved, feedback	Passive consumer behaviour
A political learning process	Depoliticization
Collective production	Production by specialists
Social control by self-organization	Control by property owners or bureaucracy

tory culture. Then follows a discussion of two (potential) obstacles to the realization of the potentialities: the possibility of hegemonic (counter)dominance, and the capitalist reality of competition and exclusion.

Colonies of Enthusiasts

There is a parallel between the notion of subculture within cultural studies and the concept of virtual community in Internet studies. Much like subcultures are aggregates of individuals coming together to create something new and to challenge established ways of seeing and doing things, virtual communities are based on the "power of cooperation" and "a merger of knowledge capital, social capital, and communion" (Rheingold, 1994, p. 109). Virtual communities attract "colonies of enthusiasts" because the digital platforms enable them "to do things with each other in new ways, and to do altogether new kinds of things" (Rheingold, 1994, p. xxi). A key aspect of this is the development and application of what Lévy (1999) calls "collective intelligence." This concept is based on the idea that no one knows everything, but everyone knows something, and that this fact can be harnessed through digital media. People being networked and sharing things results in a form of intelligence that, according to Lévy, is universally distributed, coordinated in real time, and constantly enhanced. This leads to an effective mobilization of skills. Digital culture potentially makes us members of a shared virtual universe of knowledge, the common fostering of which will make the social tie the most important currency in future society. Collective intelligence, Lévy argues, can disrupt the power of government and lead to a diversification of knowledge and desire.

Power, according to Lévy, "is now conferred through the optimal management of knowledge whether it involves technology, science, communication, or our 'ethical' relationship with the other" (1999, p. 1). We will increasingly witness the development of "skill zones that are fluid, delocalized, based on the singularities, and agitated by permanent molecular movements of association and rivalry" (p. 5). The utopian result will be a form of real-time democracy, where knowledge is no longer "padlocked like a treasure" but instead "pervades everything, is distributed, mediatized, spreads innovation wherever it is found" (p. 212).

We will now look at four overlapping concepts that align well with Lévy's theory to detail the fluid skill zones he describes: Rouse's (1991) notion of "media circuits," as adapted by Lange (2008); Jones' (1997) concept of "virtual settlements"; Wenger's (1998) idea of "communities of practice"; and Gee's (2005) construct of "affinity spaces." Some of these are conceptualizations of how the zones are formed and structured, while others provide a terminology for the collaborative activities going on within them once they have been established. The conceptual redundancy—there are certainly more semi-synonyms to be found out there—is symptomatic of the field. A lot of effort is made to name processes and patterns of online connection and engagement. It is natural for a wide array of conceptualizations to emerge in relation to new processes, and an attempt to bring the variety of overlapping theories together is needed.

Lange, for starters, uses the concept of *media circuits* to understand how networks of relations are created, maintained, and negotiated in public social media arenas. Her discussion is based on Rouse's (1991) writings about Mexican immigrants, which contain key ideas that can be translated for use in analyses of how a sense of community is established in the online context. In a world marked by the dissolution of "the comforting modern imagery" of coherent social units and communities, there is a crisis, Rouse argues, in spatial representation. A new cartography is emerging where previous notions of community and of center versus periphery are called into question. Lange implies that there are similarities between the spatial strategies of the migrants in Rouse's study and virtual groups, or "settlements," established in the digital. Both are forging spatial arrangements that transcend physical space in the sense that "important kin and friends are as likely to be living hundreds or thousands of miles away as immediately around them" (Rouse, 1991, p. 13). What is most important here is that these long-distance relationships are maintained to the same degree as—or even more so than—connections to local friends and acquaintances. Furthermore, these circuits tend to become so closely knit that they eventually can be said to constitute one single community spread across a variety of physical places. The places of communities are increasingly becoming nothing but sites where flows of communication intersect with each other and with physically situated practices.

Also employing the notion of settlements, Jones (1997) attempts to theoretically outline how a "cyber-archaeology" of virtual communities might be carried out with the help of the notion of *virtual settlements*. He writes:

> In a similar fashion, traditional human settlements have been characterized by archaeologists who have been interested in such issues as the development of sedentism, agrarian-based urban settlements and the growth of industrially based cities. In both archaeology and the field of

CMC [computer-mediated communication], researchers focus on cultural artifacts: the archaeologist on scarabs, pots, arrow heads, the remains of cities, etc., the CMC researcher on listserv postings, web site structures, web site content, number of spams, Usenet content, etc. These artifacts can provide an integrative framework for a settlement's life, be it virtual or real, or they can obstruct or fail to facilitate otherwise viable, active behavior. (Jones, 1997, section 2, n.p.)

In Jones' taxonomy, an online space where group communication happens has to meet four basic conditions to be labeled a virtual settlement: "(1) a minimum level of interactivity; (2) a variety of communicators; (3) a virtual common-public-space where a significant portion of interactive group-CMCs occur; [and] (4) a minimum level of sustained membership." This corresponds to three general questions. First, is there a common discursive code, as opposed to fragmented communication? Second, is there a social order, as opposed to random connections between users? And, finally, is there commitment over time? Once a virtual settlement has been identified, it can be made the object of empirical analysis in order to characterize the size, stability, and cohesiveness of its population. Jones suggests that such an assessment can be made on the basis of a number of factors: the number of discussion topics emerging over a particular time period, the number of participants, the average length of contributions, and so on.

A concept that can be used to describe the activities going on in media circuits or virtual settlements is provided by the theory of *communities of practice*. Originating in theories of learning, the idea of the role of joint practice in building community is also relevant to digital culture and has been widely cited in this field. The concept refers to the informal groups that people form over time through shared enterprises. Wenger describes three aspects of this relation. First, there needs to be mutual engagement among participants. Practice is not an abstract phenomenon, but something that comes into being as people engage in actions, the meanings of which they negotiate collaboratively. A community of practice is "not just an aggregate of people" (Wenger, 1998, p. 74) but the result of active interaction and meaning-making. Second, communities of practice are marked by a joint enterprise. This enterprise is the result of collective negotiation and represents the participants' response to their situation, which in turn creates relations of mutual accountability.

Finally, communities of practice entail the development of a shared repertoire. By synchronizing the resources for negotiating meaning, the participants

construct coherence in "the medley of activities, relations, and objects involved" (Wenger, 1998, p. 82). This repertoire is synonymous with the discourse in relation to which meaningful utterances and actions are made and
performed by participants. In Bourdieu's (1977b) terms, this is the "doxa" of
the "field." So, for a community of practice to develop, there has to be a component of people doing things together, establishing and maintaining relationships. There also has to be a social complexity and elements of community
maintenance. Furthermore, there needs to be some sort of joint enterprise that
is collectively negotiated and marked by mutual accountability. Finally, there
must be a shared repertoire of stories, styles and concepts. With these steps, a
community of practice is constituted through the engagement of participants.

A related way of understanding how the spatially fragmented media circuits,
settlements or communities of practice can be held together socially is from the
perspective of Gee's (2005) writings on *affinity spaces*. Rather than "communities" to which people "belong" as "members," Gee suggests that we talk of spaces
of affinity in order to capture current forms of social affiliation. By referring to
spaces instead of communities, one can go on to ask whether people who interact
in a given space form a community or not; the answer will differ from case to
case (or person to person). To Gee, affinity spaces are an especially common social form in digital culture. In these spaces, people come together because of common endeavors or interest, rather than on the basis of broader categorizations
such as nationality, ethnicity, class, gender, disability, and so on. In affinity spaces,
newcomers and masters all share the same locality, and the creation, exchange,
and distribution of knowledge is an important part of the common activities.

In sum, the disruptive spaces described at the outset of this chapter may be
conceptualized in many ways: as media circuits, as virtual settlements, as communities of practice, or as affinity spaces. Though they come from different
fields of inquiry and have been formulated based on different, specific motivations, all of these notions have a number of things in common. They are all
examples of what Lévy calls "fluid skill zones." They all have a certain degree
of fluidity stemming from their digital and sometimes global character, and
they all revolve around generating or fostering certain forms of skills or knowledge. This may be anything from the skill to efficiently encode a video file
using free software or write a short story in accordance with certain conventions of fan fiction, to the ability to coordinate a street protest or gain access
to classified government documents.

Lévy also provides a hopeful description of how the power of these skills
can be brought together to form a unified knowledge sphere that may function

as a counterforce to dominant knowledge regimes. According to Castells (2007, p. 248), the rise of the new form of networked and socialized communication, which he calls "mass self-communication," makes possible "the unlimited diversity and the largely autonomous origin of most of the communication flows that construct, and reconstruct every second the global and local production of meaning in the public mind." In relation to this, Lévy's utopian notion of "cosmopedia" represents the meta-level that might tie the otherwise isolated islands together. The cosmopedia makes available "to the collective intellect all of the pertinent knowledge available to it at a given moment, but it also serves as a site of collective discussion, negotiation, and development" (Lévy, 1999, p. 217). A similar notion is the "hive mind," as discussed and critiqued by Lanier (2010). Although this argument seems a bit abstract, and also raises questions about whether the translation of seemingly different forms of skills and knowledge is universal and unproblematic, Jenkins (2006, p. 257) provides a similar argument:

> Right now, we are learning how to apply these new participatory skills through our relation to commercial entertainment—or more precisely, right now some groups of early adopters are testing the waters and mapping out directions where many more of us are apt to follow. These skills are being applied to popular culture first [. . .]. Yet, [these skills] may quickly get applied to political activism or education or the workplace.

Such a cosmopedic translation and pooling of skills among different fields and groups is also made possible through the alleged power of *smart mobs* (Rheingold, 2002). This notion refers to the mechanism within today's highly mobile digital culture whereby participants in interest groups or manifestations use portable devices to disseminate and receive information on what to do and where to go. Smart mobs are "mobile ad hoc social networks" (Rheingold, 2002, p. 169) that are made possible, Rheingold argues, through a combination of computation, communication, reputation and location awareness. He continues:

> The *mobile* aspect is already self-evident to urbanites who see the early effects of mobile phones and SMS. *Ad hoc* means that the organizing among people and their devices is done informally and on the fly, the way texting youth everywhere coordinate meetings after school. *Social network* means that every individual in a smart mob is a "node" in the jargon of social

network analysis, with social "links" (channels of communication and social bonds) to other individuals. Nodes and links, the elements of communication networks made by humans, are also the fundamental
elements of communication networks constructed from optical cables and
wireless devices—one reason why new communication technologies
make possible profound social changes. (Rheingold, 2002, p. 170)

Descriptions such as these are deeply rooted in discourse surrounding *Web 2.0*
technologies. According to O'Reilly (2007), this concept refers to a new type
of web replacing Web 1.0 during the first years of the twenty-first century. Web
2.0 is a platform, rather than a mere channel of communication, characterized
by its focus on "harnessing collective intelligence"(O'Reilly, 2007, p. 22) and
"the wisdom of crowds" (p. 24).

But Web 2.0 is not only about technology, but also about a certain kind of
approach and ethos. Gauntlett (2011, pp. 8–13) argues that it marks a shift in
digital media use from a "sit back and be told culture" to a "making and doing
culture." At the core of Web 2.0 are a wide variety of easy-to-use and accessi-
ble online tools that enable self-publication, collaboration, informal learning
and creativity. This development is closely related to the emergence online of
what Jenkins et al. define as *participatory culture*:

> A participatory culture is a culture with relatively low barriers to artistic
> expression and civic engagement, strong support for creating and sharing
> one's creations, and some type of informal mentorship whereby what is
> known by the most experienced is passed along to novices. A participa-
> tory culture is also one in which members believe their contributions
> matter, and feel some degree of social connection with one another (at
> the least, they care what other people think about what they have cre-
> ated). (Jenkins, Clinton et al., 2009, p. 3)

This idea about an emergent cultural climate where consumers and citizens
are invited and enabled to create and circulate their own content is furthermore related to the theories of *prosumption* and *produsage*. In recent literature
developing Toffler's (1980) notion of the prosumer, Ritzer and Jurgenson
(2010) claim that Web 2.0 has facilitated the implosion of production and
consumption. They also claim that the combination of production and consumption—key elements of traditional capitalism—into the social type of the
prosumer has brought capitalism into a new phase. Ritzer and Jurgenson argue

that prosumers are more difficult to control and exploit than producers or consumers, and that there is "a greater likelihood of resistance on the part of prosumers" (2010, p. 31). The related notion of produsage (2008) is also based on the argument that Web 2.0 will have a strong transformative impact on society, through the rise of processes in which user-led content creation will play an ever more important role. Similar processes discussed by Benkler (2006), who uses the term *peer production*, and by a research group headed by Varnelis (2008) employing the label *networked publics*:

> The term *networked publics* references a linked set of social, cultural, and technological developments that have accompanied the growing engagement with digitally networked media. The Internet has not completely changed the media's role in society: mass media, or one-to-many communications, continue to cater to a wide arena of cultural life. What has changed are the ways in which people are networked and mobilized with and through media. The term *networked publics* is an alternative to terms such as *audience* or *consumer*. Rather than assume that everyday media engagement is passive or consumptive, the term *publics* foregrounds a more engaged stance. Networked publics takes this further; now publics are communicating more and more through complex networks that are bottom-up, top-down, as well as side-to-side. Publics can be reactors, (re)makers and (re)distributors, engaging in shared culture and knowledge through discourse and social exchange as well as through acts of media reception. (Ito, 2008, pp. 2–3)

At the core of this conceptual superfluity lies the argument that the power of fluid skill zones (known by many names) could be harnessed and amplified through some form of connection (also known by many names).

Empowering Some While Disempowering Others

The ideas discussed above represent the first steps in developing a perspective on what the disruptive spaces might be. Whether they are about interfering with dominant meanings in the fields of art, media, or confrontational politics, they all rely on people connecting with each other and developing various forms of common knowledge and skills. But many of these perspectives have been questioned for being overly optimistic about the democratizing and participatory potential of digital platforms. Critics have argued that such "cyber-optimism," rooted in the early Internet studies of Rheingold, Jenkins, and others, is "partisan and dated" (Kahn & Kellner, 2008, p. 22), and that we must focus on critical evaluation of the actual nature, effects, and possibilities of disruptive spaces. Although the notion of the cosmopedia is compelling, it remains utopian, and what we can do today is look for any traces of cosmopedic connections between isolated skill zones that potentially represent the beginnings of a more coherent challenge to dominant ideologies.

While concepts such as "collective intelligence" may be useful for describing parts of what goes on in wikis and discussion forums, and while notions of "communities of practice" or "affinity spaces" may be well-suited for describing emerging patterns in the fields of informal learning or fan culture, there is a danger in drawing on ideas like this when making general statements about society, culture, history, and the state of the public sphere in today's societies. Jenkins (2006, p. 290) writes that while he believes "very firmly in the potential for participatory culture to serve as a catalyst for revitalizing civic life, we still fall short of the full realization of those ideals." And, certainly, as Gauntlett (2011, pp. 185–216) discusses, there may be reason to believe that the world of Web 2.0 is "not all rosy." Various forms of engagement via the net are sometimes condescendingly labeled *slacktivism* (Christensen, 2011; Morozov, 2011) or *clicktivism* (White, 2010). Perspectives on collective intelligence, participatory culture, and the like are attacked for being cyber-utopian, techno-determinist, naïvely optimistic, and so on. This may be partly because many of these arguments have been adopted by journalists, PR people, and entrepreneurs. While there is nothing wrong with that as such, it has led to a certain watering-down of the original scholarly concepts and a backgrounding of the important criticisms of many researchers in the field.

Morozov (2011, p. xvii) takes the criticism to the macro level by pointing out that those "who still care about the future of democracy will need to ditch both cyber-utopianism and Internet-centrism," as well as "today's quasi-religious discourse about the power of the Internet" (p. 276). In Lovink's words, perspectives that "present the Internet as a holy thing, ultimately connecting all human synapses" (2005, p. 5) need to be replaced by approaches that attempt a critical assessment of its promises. Morozov underlines the problem with interpreting all forms of online creativity and community-building as evidence that major sociocultural transformations are under way. There is a difference, he argues, between apolitical and political contexts. So, returning to Jenkins' argument that what goes on in popular culture can be translated into "more serious matters," this is not necessarily true. Morozov draws a parallel with the proven power of social media during natural disasters:

> [T]he reason why many projects that rely on crowdsourcing produce trustworthy data in natural disasters is because those are usually apolitical events. There are no warring sides, and those who report data do not have any incentive to manipulate it. The problem with using such crowdsourced tools for other purposes [...] is that the accuracy of such reports is impossible to verify and easy to manipulate. (Morozov, 2011, p. 271)

Before celebrating social media such as Twitter or Facebook for their potential to overcome differences and bring people together, we must consider the possibility that differences and conflict may in fact be accentuated by these same media. For example, Morozov contends, nationalism is being revived on the Internet. The idea that increased access to technology equals more democracy is a fallacy that needs to be debunked. While digital tools obviously have the potential to promote democracy, it is vital to realize that these same platforms also have rendered more powerful those who oppose democratization. Referring to Doppelt (2001), Morozov underlines that any specific case of technopolitics must be evaluated in relation to the specific group of users, their motivations, and the sociopolitical context. If we do not ask such questions, we will come to the conclusion, Morozov writes, "that the blogging Al-Qaeda is good for democracy, because blogs have opened up new and cheap vistas for public participation" (2011, p. 265). One must keep in mind that new technologies will always empower some while disempowering others. Technology is merely a tool that can be used for many purposes depending on who is using it, why, where, and when. Morozov (2011, pp. 315–320), not unlike Lovink (2002) and Kahn and Kellner (2008), argues for a "cyber-realism" that accepts that digital platforms will produce different political outcomes in different environments.

Fuchs (2008) argues that the starting point for understanding the Internet is looking at it from the perspective of self-organizing systems. He writes that the true essence of society could be realized through grassroots processes of social cooperation and self-organization. But this potential is not automatically realized, because there are "neoliberal understandings of self-organization that want to deprive humans of their agency in order to legitimate the domination of capitalist structures that colonize society" (Fuchs, 2008, p. 34). As society is dominated by class formation, competition, and accumulation, there is an antagonism between cooperation and competition obstructing the realization of the collaborative potentials. This dialectic, Fuchs claims, sits at the very core of informational capitalism, producing tensions between proprietary space and open space. Still, he identifies a radical possibility:

> Global network capitalism has created novel methods and qualities of domination and competition, but at the same time it has advanced new opportunities for cooperation and participation that question domination and point towards alternative futures. It is an antagonistic space that by producing new networks of domination also produces potential networks of liberation that undermine the centralization of wealth and power. (Fuchs, 2008, pp. 119–120)

These potential networks that can possibly undermine domination could be conceptualized as disruptive spaces, underlining the fact that their attempts to subvert are never successful in any automatic way just because the attempts are made with the help of digital technologies. The "overall competitive character of contemporary society" (Fuchs, 2008, p. 138) may provide substantial obstacles to this realization. There are indeed digital divides (Castells, 2001) by which access to the Internet is unequally distributed. The ways in which different groups employ "tactical media" (Lovink, 2002, pp. 254–275) always evolve in the force field between "eDomination" and "eParticipation" (Fuchs, 2008, pp. 213–298). When trying to come to terms with the potential and effect of disruptive spaces, we must remember that cyberculture, as Fuchs argues, is a heterogeneous and dialectical system marked by struggles between cooperation and alienation: "Under given societal conditions, cyberspace is both a tool for the reinforcement and shrinking of sociability" (Fuchs, 2008, p. 333).

Realizing this, we must use the terms *participatory culture*, *prosumption*, and *prosumerism* very carefully. The significance of concepts such as these is exaggerated in much Web 2.0 discourse. As shown by Fuchs (2011), this discourse lacks a developed theoretical reasoning about what participation actually means. Participation, he argues, is "an inherently normative concept that has political implications" (2011, p. 290), and any arguments that Web 2.0 is participatory must be well-grounded. The key point here is that the actual effect and workings of any digital tool much be evaluated with reference to the context. Fuchs summarizes:

My argument is that Web 2.0 has contradictory, dialectical *potentials* for society, both positive ones (such as the advancement of civil society, public discourse, active prosumptive media usage by the masses, more open discursive and democratic forms of education and the commons as new model of common democratic ownership) and negative ones (such as the corporate appropriation of Web 2.0, digital exclusion and digital divides, the exploitation of Internet prosumers, the fragmentation of the public sphere and the creation of an e-literate online elite) that contradict and encroach each other. (Fuchs, 2011, pp. 290–291)

As pointed out by Fuchs, this argument is in parallel to Castells' (2009) idea that allegedly participatory platforms may be used as tools for commodification as well as counter-power.

Technopolitics: Towards a Continuous Re-theorization

This potential for counter-power is dealt with by Kahn and Kellner (2008), who use the term *technopolitics* for the emerging type of politics that is mediated through a wide range of digital tools and platforms. While retaining a critical perspective, they contend that a set of "online activist subcultures" and political groups that have materialized during the first part of the twenty-first century function as "a vital oppositional space of politics and culture in which a wide diversity of individuals and groups have used emergent technologies to help produce creative social relations and forms of democratic political possibility" (2008, p. 34). Kahn and Kellner contend that many of these groups have been appropriated by the mainstream and thus rendered harmless through the capitalist processes described by Fuchs, but they also predict the emergence of novel oppositional cultures and alternative voices—disruptive spaces. They write:

Examples of oppositional use of emergent technologies have been regularly occurring with the anti-corporate globalization, anti-war, and progressive social movements, and all of these together demonstrate that while it is significant to criticize the ways in which emergent media ecologies can serve as one-dimensionalizing environments, it is equally necessary to examine the ways in which everyday people subvert the in-

tended uses of these media tools (and so those that produce them) towards their own needs and uses. (Kahn & Kellner, 2008, p. 25)

In order to study these patterns, Kahn and Kellner draw on McLuhan's (1964)
idea of media as constantly evolving environments where new media and
technologies appear all the time. They suggest using the notion of "media
ecologies" to grasp the continued growth of the Internet and the steady evolution of new gadgets and applications as a multidimensional set of tools for
organizing new types of interaction. They argue that the technopolitics of
emergent media ecologies must be continuously retheorized and critically assessed. Furthermore, they provide a perspective that combines the utopian
hopefulness of the most optimistic advocates of the participatory culture perspective and the dystopian skepticism of its harshest critics. In other words,
they identify the same double potential as Fuchs, but are a little bit more optimistic about the possibilities for counter-power to emerge under the current
social conditions.

> Yet, we do not mean to imply that the technopolitics [. . .] are essentially,
> or even mostly, participatory and democratic. We recognize major com-
> mercial interests at play and that emergent technologies are presently
> the site of a struggle [. . . .] Recognizing the many ways in which politics
> become limited as it implodes into technoculture, we therefore want to
> engage in dialectical critique of how emergent types of information and
> communication technologies (ICTs) have facilitated oppositional cul-
> tural and political movements and provided possibilities for the sort of
> progressive social change and struggle that is an important dimension of
> contemporary cultural politics. (Kahn & Kellner, 2008, p. 23)

By this, they mean that although technopolitics may facilitate cultural and
political disruption from below, the realization of this potential cannot be
taken for granted. Once again, this leads us to the conclusion that instead of
speculating further about whether digital media may—at a philosophical
level—bring about a transformation of society, we must look at actual and contextualized circumstances.

· 2 ·

IN SEARCH OF SPACE

Whatever code we hack, be it programming language, poetic language,
math or music, curves or colourings, we create the possibility of new
things entering the world. (Wark, 2004, n.p.)

According to Jones (1994, p. 17) "computer-mediated communication is, in essence, socially produced space." This book is about the study of digital culture, with a focus on the types of spaces it enables. In the previous chapter, "disruptive spaces" were conceptualized as sites of struggle where structure and hegemony can constrain agency and resistance. But at the same time, they also form the basis for the development of tactics for coping with, evading, or resisting oppressive and limiting forces. Perspectives on disruptive spaces risk falling into either technophilia or technophobia.

Digital media tools and platforms may be a major force to be reckoned with as they enable different forms of revolutionary or rebellious activities in areas ranging from art and culture to piracy and politics. Yet, although it has long been assumed that digital media has a liberatory potential, technologies as such do not have decided outcomes inscribed in them. We turn therefore to the empirical questions regarding disruptive spaces: What, precisely, are these spaces? What do they do, and with what specific contextualized effects? What characterizes the disruptive spaces, and how might they be understood in relation to the wider framework of hegemony and resistance, publics and counterpublics? In order to be able to answer these questions, an analytical strategy is needed.

The previous chapter demonstrated that the potentially disruptive spaces of digital culture are seen in quite different ways by different researchers and theorists. Generally, there is an optimistic "participatory" strand and another more pessimistic "critical" strand. Conceptualizations of how groups— "colonies of enthusiasts," "virtual communities"—are formed in digital culture were introduced in chapter 1. The role of knowledge production and collective intelligence in these processes was addressed in discussion of concepts such as "media circuits," "virtual settlements," "communities of practice," "affinity spaces," and "smart mobs." These are semi-synonymous concepts, overlapping to varying degrees, that all suggest ways of conceptualizing patterns of online connection and engagement. Lévy's notion of "fluid skill zones" was used as an umbrella concept for all of them.

The "cosmopedia" and the "hive mind" were introduced as examples of theories that point out possibilities for how the power of various circuits/settlements/communities/spaces might be brought together, harnessed, and channeled to provide a counter-hegemonic challenge. I introduced the concepts of "participatory culture," "prosumerism," and "produsage" as examples of how the power of fluid skill zones has been explained. We then turned to a discussion of the downside of interpreting participatory culture and fluid skill zones as great social force that will transform society at its very basis.

Many scholars agree that development in that direction will not happen automatically, or without friction. It was highlighted, with reference to the writings of Morozov, that these same tools and platforms can just as easily be used—and are already being used—for destructive and oppressive purposes. Technologies as such do not have any decided outcomes inscribed in them. To further emphasize the difference between the theoretical potential and the realized potential of digital media, we turned to Fuchs' discussion of the antagonisms within cyberculture between domination and liberation, and between competition and collaboration. A review of the scholarly texts produced by proponents of the various perspectives reveals that the unifying points are not as few as is sometimes claimed, but this is not to say that there are no differences. As Gramsci (1971) argues, hegemonic rule is a "moving equilibrium," and dominance has to be continuously won, reproduced, and sustained.

As the context of disruptive spaces is caught up in the complex reality of technology (mediated by protocol at the level of code) and communication (mediated by discourse at the level of language), embedded in social relations (as established via digital media), all three of these dimensions must be dealt with in order to arrive at a design for studying these spaces. This chapter will develop an analytical framework of disruptive spaces as practice—as intersections of protocol, discourse, and social relations. The technological, cultural, and social aspects of the Internet cannot be dealt with in isolation from each other.

Interference in the Orderly Sequence

Disruptive spaces, if and when their potential is realized, may function as part of a positive development that makes possible a wider range of opinions, new modes of making sense of social reality, and new forms for creativity, as well as direct activism. Disruptive spaces are the latent building blocks of a tentative alternative public sphere—a counterpublic. Under the best of circumstances, if they are appropriated efficiently, disruptive spaces can "make possible a reconfiguring of politics and culture and a refocusing of participatory democratic politics for everyday life" (Kahn & Kellner, 2008, p. 33). Disruptive spaces may, in other words, optimally resist dominant ways of doing things and of conceiving of social reality. In those cases, they can represent what traditional cultural studies calls a "subcultural challenge." But the notion of subculture needs to be rethought for the digital era.

Any culture, any prevailing regime for living and conceiving of reality, might be questioned and challenged from within. This is, for example, what piracy does with the copyright paradigm, what remix culture does with the notion of authorship, and what digital grassroots activism does with traditional systems of political representation. They all aim, more or less explicitly and directly, to challenge established models for how things are and how they should function. When dominant frameworks and commonsensical stances are somehow subjected to this type of interference or disruption, and when these disturbances have a certain coherence and perseverance, we can speak of subcultures. These are cultures within cultures, and they are constituted on the basis of providing some sort of critique of or alternative to the status quo. Subcultures may be overtly political, or rooted in subversive activities that are political in a more indirect sense. What unifies subcultures is that they "represent 'noise' (as opposed to sound): interference in the orderly sequence" (Hebdige, 1979, p. 90).

Hebdige (1979) argues that the power of subculture is "an actual mechanism of semantic disorder: a kind of temporary blockage in the system of representation" (p. 90). Subcultures operate to destroy existing codes and to formulate new ones through appropriations, thefts, and subversive transformations (p. 129). They are warnings to the "straight world" of the presence of difference, and they signal a refusal through their power to disfigure. In this argument, all disruptions are somehow semantic or symbolic (see chapter 3 for further discussion).

Hebdige argues that subcultures represent the types of objections and contradictions that Lefebvre (1971) describes as obstructions to closing the ideological circuit between sign and object. Subcultures interrupt the process of "normalization" (Barthes, 1972), detaching themselves from "the taken-for-granted landscape" (Hebdige, 1979, p. 19). By emitting noise in the form of symbolical challenges, subcultures make obvious the continuities and breaks between subordinate and dominant value systems. Melucci (1996) writes about this in terms of challenging hegemonic codes through attempts to reverse the symbolic order. This book is rooted in the social constructionist idea that even though material and very real realities exist in people's lives, it is at the level of code, language, discourse, and signification that they are loaded with meanings that may function in limiting or enabling ways, and that may be reproduced or resisted (Bourdieu, 1991; Burr, 2003; Fairclough, 1989).

Culture, according to Williams (1961), should be seen as a particular way of life based on specific meanings and values that affect art, learning, institutions, and behavior. From that perspective, cultural analysis is about clarifying which meanings and values are explicit and implicit in a specific way of life—a specific culture. As argued by Althusser (1969), Barthes (1972), and Hall (1997), every culture carries with it a rhetoric of common sense. Naturalized mythologies and dominant ideologies give the ideas of "how things are" a seemingly spontaneous and natural quality that resists any change or correction. Gramsci's (1971) notion of hegemony provides an account of how such dominant discourses about reality—which legitimize the interests of the dominant groups in society—are sustained. It all happens through an uneven negotiation that results in the manufacture of consent.

Hegemony, however, will only prevail as long as the dominant groups succeed in disarming any competing definitions of reality. Against this background, subcultures represent those systems of meanings and values that resist the mythological and ideological notions of how things are, and should be. The study of subculture is the study of these challenges, these disruptions, this noise. Furthermore, we must always speak of cultures as well as subcultures in the plural.

> The dominant culture of a complex society is never a homogenous structure. It is layered, reflecting different interests within the dominant class, containing different traces from the past, as well as emergent elements in the present. Subordinate cultures will not always be in open conflict with it. They may, for long periods, coexist with it, negotiate the spaces and gaps in it, make inroads into it [. . . .] [I]t is crucial to replace the notion of "culture" with the more concrete, historical concept of "cultures"; a redefinition which brings out more clearly the fact that cultures always stand in relations of domination—and subordination— to one another, [and] are always, in some sense, in struggle with one another. (Clarke, Hall, Jefferson, & Roberts, 1975, p. 12)

The concept of subculture was introduced long before Hebdige's contribution (Gelder, 2005; Gordon, 1947; Lee, 1945), and because it has been employed and reworked in a number of contexts throughout the years while society has changed significantly, some writers feel that it has now "run its course" (Jenks, 2005, p. 145). Others think it should retain its significance if it is adjusted according to "post-subcultural" models (Bennett & Kahn-Harris, 2004; Muggleton & Weinzierl, 2003). The idea of subculture emerged to describe monolithic social relations and clear-cut distinctions in a historical context with few and clearly discernable arenas of conflict, but late modern culture has brought about significant changes in this respect, particularly through the development of the Internet and social media and the ongoing fragmentation, specialization, and compartmentalization of the public and the social. The notion of subculture, in its previous form, is becoming increasingly redundant as "the type of investment that the notion of subculture labeled is becoming more general, and therefore the varieties of modes of symbolization and involvement are more common" (Chaney, 2004, p. 37).

In today's increasingly diverse cultures, vocabularies of cultural taste and social action are highly differentiated, meaning that a much larger heterogeneity of identities, styles, and values can be adopted by individuals who are still seen as "ordinary people" and part of the mainstream. In short, "the qualities of appropriation and innovation once applied to subcultures can be seen in re-lation to a range of consumer and leisure-based groupings across the social spectrum" (Chaney, 2004, p. 41). These more fluid differentiations are by no means a sign that structural conflicts have disappeared: Cultural conflicts over how things are and should be still exist, and they are still "political in every tissue of their being" (Chaney, 2004, p. 47). The difference is that in a frag-mented culture, clashes between conformity and diversity must be conceptu-alized with new and more sophisticated metaphors, and the consequences of this fragmentation for the power of subculture must be problematized. This is especially true for the study of subcultural aspects of digital culture. In order to understand subcultural aspects in complex societies and fragmented cultures, we must turn to the issue of "how control exists after decentralization" (Thacker, 2004).

Opposing Machines

Galloway (2004, p. 2) starts from Deleuze's claim that every society has its di-agrams, and further explains that the diagram of the distributed network (which is characteristic of the Internet), the technology of the digital com-puter, and the management style of protocol are key to explaining the sociopo-litical logics of the present age. He defines protocol as the underlying code or language "that regulates flow, directs netspace, codes relationships, and con-nects lifeforms" (p. 244).

While centralized networks are ordered around one single authoritative hub, and as decentralized networks consist of many hubs that all have their own sets of dependent nodes, the Internet is a *distributed network* where each node may connect to any other node, even if it is not required to. Using Deleuze and Guattari's (1987) concept, these networks are *rhizomatic*, mean-ing that they resist any hierarchic description. The emergence of this type of network marks a more general societal shift (Galloway, 2004, p. 32). There is a movement into an increasingly (hyper)connected age (Christakis & Fowler, 2010) in which the focus shifts from networks as pure structure to the idea that networks are "actually *doing something*" (Watts, 2003, p. 28).

Galloway (2004) formulates his theory of protocol for grasping the processes and mechanisms that underpin the workings of the Internet. He underlines the importance of moving in the direction of network analysis in order to "understand how social change is indissociable from technological development [...] though not determined by it" (Thacker, 2004, p. xii). A foundation of this understanding is, in turn, an understanding of the technological aspects of the Internet and the consequences of its social and political uses. The Internet is highly flexible and adaptable—its protocols are "the enemy of bureaucracy, of rigid hierarchy, and of centralization" (Galloway, 2004, p. 29)—and this is the result of a specific historical process.

In 1959, at the height of the Cold War, Paul Baran, a computer scientist at the RAND Corporation, a U.S. military think tank, was given the task of creating a communications system able to withstand a nuclear attack. The strategy was to establish a computer network that did not rely on centralized command and thus was not vulnerable to attacks targeting central hubs (Barabási, 2002, pp. 143–145; Galloway, 2004, pp. 4–5). Baran's network was based on the technology of packet-switching, by which messages are distributed in small fragments to be reassembled at the receiving end. The system was finally realized at the end of the 1960s with the establishment of the Advanced Research Projects Agency (ARPA), President Eisenhower's response to the Soviet Sputnik launch. The agency's ARPANET, the first computer network based on packet-switching, was used by the military and by academics to transfer and exchange information (Barabási, 2002, pp. 146–147; Galloway, 2004, p. 5). Castells (2001, pp. 24–25) describes this era:

> Graduate students played a decisive role in the design of ARPANET. In the late 1960s, the Network Working Group, which did most of the design of ARPANET's protocols, was composed mainly of graduate students, including [Vint] Cerf, [Steve] Crocker, and [Jon] Postel, who studied together in the same secondary school in Southern California, and then were students of [Leonard] Kleinrock at UCLA. Feeling insecure about their decisions, they communicated their work in progress [...] through "request for comment" memos or RFCs, which provided the style, and the name, for informal technical communication in the Internet world up to our day. The openness of this format was—and continues to be—essential for the development of the Internet's infrastructure protocols. Most of these students were not countercultural in the sense of the social movements' activists of the time. Cerf certainly was not. They were too obsessed with their extraordinary technological adventure to see much of the world outside computers. They certainly did not see any

problem in having their research funded by the Pentagon or even in joining ARPA (as Cerf did) in the midst of the Vietnam War. And yet they were permeated with the values of individual freedom, of independent thinking, and of sharing and cooperation with their peers, all values that characterized the campus culture of the 1960s. While the young ARPANETers were not part of the counterculture, their ideas, and their software, provided a natural bridge between the world of big science and the broader student culture that sprung up in the BBSs and Usenet News network. This student culture took up computer networking as a tool of free communication, and in the case of its most political manifestations (Nelson, Jennings, Stallman), as a tool of liberation, which, together with the PC, would provide people with the power of information to free themselves both from governments and corporations.

These grassroots, as Castells calls them, had a great impact on how the global Internet emerged out of ARPANET. He writes that the Internet was "born at the unlikely intersection of big science, military research and libertarian culture" (2001, p. 17). Although its developers were not countercultural, and many of them were "content with just fostering good computer science," the project "was rooted in a scientific dream to change the world through computer communication" that "had little to do with military strategy" (p. 19). Control of the central "backbone" of the network was transferred from the Department of Defense to the National Science Foundation in 1988, and then to commercial telecommunications interests in 1995 (Galloway, 2004, p. 6). The creation of a number of protocols has been crucial for the continued development of the Internet and the World Wide Web, an information-sharing application developed in the early 1990s by the English programmer Tim Berners-Lee. Galloway (2004, p. 39) explains: "In order for hosts to communicate via the Internet, they must implement an entire suite of different protocols. Protocols are the common languages that all computers on the network speak." The information age, according to him, is not only the age of computers, but the age in which "protocol becomes the controlling force in social life" (Galloway, 2004, p. 111).

> At the core of networked computing is the concept of *protocol*. [...] For example, many of the protocols used on the World Wide Web (a network within the Internet) are governed by the World Wide Web Consortium (WC3) [that] was created in October 1994 to develop common

protocols such as Hypertext Markup Language (HTML) and Cascading Style Sheets. Scores of other protocols have been created for a variety of other purposes by many different professional societies and organizations. (Galloway, 2004, pp. 6–7)

In digital computing, the term *protocol* refers to specific standards for implementing specific technologies. Protocol establishes the "essential points necessary to enact an agreed-upon standard of action" (Galloway, 2004, p. 7). Referring to the relationship between the protocols of TCP/IP and DNS, Galloway suggests that the Internet rests on "a *contradiction* between two opposing machines" (Galloway, 2004, p. 8). He writes, "one protocol [TCP/IP] radically distributes control into autonomous agents, the other [DNS] rigidly organizes control into a tree-like centralized database" (Galloway, 2004, p. 53). This insight—which means that entire countries or continents may be removed from the Web with the stroke of a delete key by someone controlling a root server—makes it obvious that the Internet is anything by uncontrollable. Even though its distributed network structure marks an attempt at the level of code and technology to eliminate hierarchies, the Internet is still structured around control and command. This has led to the emergence of what Galloway (2004, p. 13) labels "counter-protocological forces." These counterforces are radiating out of the disruptive spaces that were the focus of discussion in the previous chapter. In other words, the potential of disruptive spaces is a counter-protocological one.

In line with the duality between "optimistic" and "pessimistic" perspectives on the realization of the potentials of digital media, Galloway (2004) also describes the Internet as deceptive. Protocol will by necessity involve a complex set of forces, some reactionary, some progressive. He writes of the familiar exclamations that everything has changed, and that there will now be unprecedented opportunities for diversification, personal freedom, greater choice, and free expression. His own position, however, is that these exclamations need to be examined further (p. 61). While the Web mirrors several key characteristics of the rhizome, it is neither without center, nonhierarchical, nor nonsignifying. Once again, the actual realization of its potential for participation and disruption is an empirical question that needs to be explored in context. Struggles may be lost or won "in specific places at specific times" (p. 206).

Galloway (2004, p. 150) writes of exploring "resistive strains within computer culture and how they promise to move protocol into an exciting new space." After all, protocol is synonymous with possibility, and this possibility may be realized through various tactics. Although "tactical media" has been defined as a specific aesthetic politics (Garcia & Lovink, 1997; Raley, 2009), this book adopts a more general definition, while mapping out *tactical effects* that often leave only traces of their success to be discovered later by the ecologists of the media. This might include more than would normally fit under the orthodox definition" (Galloway, 2004, p. 175). Successful tactics in network-based struggles may be performed by *liminal agents* that are "at once inside protocol and outside its reach" (p. 186). The goal of tactical media is reached if and when technology is used in ways that are "in closer agreement with the real wants and desires of its users" (p. 206).

In distinguishing between interactivity and participation, Jenkins (2006, p. 133) also uses the concept of protocols. His idea is that strictly technological aspects of certain media forms allow for differing degrees of interactivity: Reading a newspaper allows for a lesser level of interactivity than a video game in which players can act upon the world that is represented. Participation, on the other hand, does not rely on technology as such, but instead on the ways in which media use is shaped by cultural and social *protocols*. Jenkins provides no detailed descriptions of how such protocols should be analyzed. Galloway's discussion relies heavily on the role of *code* in how computers interrelate, but surely the argument can be extended into to the sphere of culture and language. Computers and the Internet are, as Galloway claims, a fundamentally textual medium. They are based on the technological language of code that renders them readable in the semiotic and discursive sense. They have a "sophisticated syntax and grammar" of their own, they "exist in specific communities and cultures," and they unite communities "through shared meaning and value" (Galloway, 2004, p. xxiv). We must therefore read the digital as one would read any text within cultural studies. And, as argued by Hands (2011, p. 87), "[p]rotocol relies initially on the same logic as all communication—that of a shared horizon of terms." Furthermore:

> What makes the web is not any one individual part but the interaction of the whole, so that the protocols are interwoven, including with the linguistic "content." To try to separate these out into discrete streams in a network makes no sense. (Hands, 2011, p. 91)

There are a number of analogies between the notions of protocol and discourse. Protocol entails established rules that "govern the set of possible behavior patterns within a heterogeneous system" (Galloway, 2004, p. 7), and is thereby a form of voluntary regulation. But while the regulations of protocol within the domain of computers operate strictly at the level of coding, we can identify here a fruitful connection to notions of discourse within poststructuralist cultural theory. Much like protocol, discourses are socially agreed-upon conventions for symbolic and material acts, the adherence to which is necessary for any act to come across as meaningful or decodable (Foucault, 1971), even if its effect is to question or reproduce dominant meanings. Furthermore, much like discourse is always connected to power, dominance, and submission, protocol is also very much about control.

Protocol and discourse are structures—rules and resources (Giddens, 1984)—enabling and limiting hegemony as well as resistance. Protocols are understood in the following discussion as the materialized and materializing codes that underlie and surround collective action in digital networks. Disruptive spaces are formed in adherence to prevailing discourse/protocol, but if their liberatory potential is realized, they might also function as resistive/counterprotocological forces.

In this book, Galloway's discussion of the workings of protocol will be extended into the sphere of social network analysis and discourse studies. The key point of Galloway's perspective in this case is that it provides a link between deeply seated operating logics of the Internet on the one hand and the workings of discourse, as described in cultural sociology, on the other. Warner (2002a, p. 50), defining the concept of *publics*, writes that a public "is a space of discourse organized by nothing other than discourse itself." To him, publics are as much conceptual and discursive as they are material: "A public is the social space created by the reflexive circulation of discourse" (p. 62). As Bourdieu (1977a, p. 647) writes: "Discourse always owes its most important characteristics to the linguistic production relations within which it is produced." Furthermore, echoing aspects of protocological relations: "Speech presupposes a legitimate transmitter addressing a legitimate receiver, one who is recognized and recognizing" (p. 649). Defining the concept of *counterpublics*, Warner writes (notably using the term *protocols*):

[A counterpublic] is a scene for developing oppositional interpretations of its members' identities, interests, and needs. They are structured by different dispositions or protocols from those that obtain elsewhere in the culture, making different assumptions about what can be said or what goes without saying. [. . .] The cultural horizon against which it marks itself off is not just a general or wider public, but a dominant one. And the

conflict extends not just to ideas or policy questions, but to the speech
genres and modes of address that constitute the public and to the hierarchy among media. (Warner, 2002a, p. 86)

This means that discourse and language must always be analyzed with reference to the social space, or the public, in relation to which they are put into
play. This is because "[l]anguage is not only an instrument of communication
or even of knowledge, but also an instrument of power. A person speaks not
only to be understood but also to be believed, obeyed, respected, distinguished" (Bourdieu, 1977a, p. 648). Much as the Internet would cease to function without protocol, language—according to Bourdieu—will function only
as long as the social field of legitimate transmitters and receivers is secured. If
the social network breaks down, so will communication. This complexity
means that in order to study discourse, one must also examine the social conditions of its production. Lefebvre (1974, p. 110) writes: "Every social space is
the outcome of a process with many aspects and many contributing currents,
signifying and non-signifying, perceived and directly experienced, practical
and theoretical."

   This book approaches the complexities of protocol, social relations, and
language by focusing its analyses on how these three dimensions intersect in
actual spaces. This is because the three cannot be analyzed in isolation, at
least not for the purpose of producing a comprehensive cultural sociology of
these settings. As argued above, protocol is inextricably entangled with discourse and language. Discourse and language, in turn, cannot be studied without also addressing the spaces of social relations in which they are used and
reproduced. This means a focus on what Bourdieu (1977b, 1990) calls the
"logic of practice."

Disruption as Heterodoxy

Bourdieu's perspective on social practice locates within social spaces the ways
in which intentions, predispositions, history, and materiality intersect in practice. When defining the very discipline of sociology as a science of the social
world, he writes:

   Initially, sociology presents itself as a *social topology*. Thus, the social
   world can be represented as a space (with several dimensions) con-

structed on the basis of principles of differentiation or distribution constituted by the set of properties active within the social universe in question, i.e., capable of conferring strength, power within that universe [. . .].
Agents and groups of agents are thus defined by their relative positions
within that space. Each of them is assigned to a position or a precise class
of neighboring positions (i.e., a particular region in this space) and one
cannot really—even if one can in thought—occupy two opposite regions
of the space. [. . .] [O]ne can also describe it as a field of forces, i.e., as a
set of objective power relations that impose themselves on all who enter
the field and that are irreducible to the intentions of the individual
agents or even to the direct interactions among the agents. (Bourdieu,
1985, pp. 723–724)

This can be directly applied to a cultural sociology of disruptive spaces, as
these spaces are situated in a wider and multidimensional social space (i.e.,
"society") where they assume positions in relation to other spatialities on the
basis of relations of power. Individuals and groups populating, and constructing, the disruptive spaces are defined by their relative positions within these
spaces. And the spaces as such are positioned in relation to other spaces. Activists as well as activism, produsers as well as produsage, remixers as well as
remixes are parts of hierarchical fields of forces on different levels of abstraction. While agents are free to act in important respects, they are also re-
stricted by powers that are irreducible to individual agents or interactions.
An individual creator may post fan fiction in a forum, but he or she must still
submit to the "rules" of the social field of this forum, and there also remains
a hierarchical order in the wider force field of texts where original texts will
still hold a stronger truth-claim than the rehashed or subverted suggestions.
An activist can tweet or blog—or throw a rock for that matter—but his or
her semiotic actions will still be judged in relation to the "doxa" of the movement. And the movement to which the activist aspires will in turn be judged
on the basis of its symbolic resources in the wider social field of the public
sphere and politics. These are the exact processes that the 99% of the Occupy
movement and the symbolic legions of the Anonymous hacktivist movement
aim to circumvent.

The three notions of rules, doxa, and symbolic resources, brought to the
fore in the previous paragraph, are key to Bourdieu's theory of practice. What
he tries to do with this conceptual system is to get beyond the long-standing
debate about structure versus agency in sociology. Can people act freely, or are

they restrained by predefined social scripts? This argument has many similarities to the debate over the power of digital media to transform society, as out-
lined in the previous chapter. While many of the more optimistic perspectives
put free individuals, saturated with agency, at the center of discourse (cf. *Time*
magazine's 2006 person of the year: "You"), the more pessimistic standpoints
tend to be based on the premise that the structural arrangements of capitalism
will tie "You" down. Bourdieu attempts to overcome this duality by introducing the idea of the *habitus*—the package of dispositions that is deposited in the
individual and that guides his or her interactions with others, or, for that matter, the predisposition of a social space in itself. The habitus is a source of
strategies that is a "generative principle of regulated improvisations" (Bourdieu, 1977b, p. 78) that "functions at every moment as a *matrix of perceptions,
appreciations, and actions*" (p. 83). Habitus must be studied through a focus on
practice, because it appears only in "the whole art of performance" (Bourdieu,
1977b, p. 20). It is "constituted in practice and is always oriented towards practical functions" (Bourdieu, 1990, p. 52).

Rules—i.e., protocol or discourse—are "themselves the product of a small
batch of schemes enabling agents to generate an infinity of practices adapted
to endlessly changing situations, without those schemes ever having been considered as explicit principles" (Bourdieu, 1990, p. 16). The rules amount up to
the doxa—the common assumptions and protocols for any given social field,
which constitutes a "universe of that which is taken for granted" (p. 170). This
universe is the result of the fact that "[e]very established order tends to produce (to very different degrees and with different means) the naturalization of
its own arbitrariness" (p. 164).

To describe tensions between hegemony and resistance, Bourdieu separates
between the notions of doxa, orthodoxy, and heterodoxy. The doxa represents
the possibility of a completely naturalized order in which "the natural and social world appears as self-evident," and through which "it seems as if there are
not multiple, but only a single possibility" (Bourdieu, 1977b, p. 164). It is a
sociocultural subtext about how the world works and ought to work, which is
unspoken and naturalized to the degree that it is "unthinkable" and beyond
opinion (p. 170). The doxa, however, may be challenged. As Bourdieu formulates it: "The truth of doxa is only fully revealed when negatively constituted
by the constitution of a field of opinion, the locus of the confrontation of competing discourses" (p. 168). As fan fiction puts Spock in bed with Kirk, as a
feminist remix video has Buffy Summers slay Edward Cullen, as Anonymous
threatens to take down the Internet to protest against capitalism, as the 99%

of the Occupy movement points out that the prevailing order serves only the remaining 1%, the doxa is questioned and denaturalized. These are all expressions of what Bourdieu calls *heterodoxy*—the articulation of alternatives to doxa. Heterodoxy, in other words, is a name for the currents flowing out of disruptive spaces. It represents a disagreement with dominant mainstream assumptions about how things should be.

Heterodoxy brings focus to the ways in which power is structured through norms, institutions, and common sense. It is thus a necessary precursor to "the awakening of political consciousness" (Bourdieu, 1977b, p. 170). As heterodox noise is emitted from somewhere, those who have an interest in keeping the doxa naturalized may respond through the assertion of "orthodoxy":

> The dominated classes have an interest in pushing back the limits of doxa and exposing the arbitrariness of the taken for granted; the dominant classes have an interest in defending the integrity of doxa or, short of this, of establishing in its place the necessarily imperfect substitute, orthodoxy. (Bourdieu, 1977b, pp. 168–169)

Orthodoxy thus substitutes for the doxa when its cover has been blown. As an imperfect replacement, it replaces the invisible coercion of the doxa with explicit strategies of control and dominance. In keeping with the idea that the symbolic cannot be analyzed in isolation from the material, Bourdieu (1985, p. 731) writes that "objective power relations tend to reproduce themselves in symbolic power relations, in views of the social world that help to ensure the permanence of these power relations." In struggles between orthodoxy and heterodoxy, agents and spaces yield "a power proportionate to their symbolic capital" (p. 731). *Symbolic capital* is Bourdieu's name for the resources deployed in such trials of strength. This capital represents the accumulated power to define reality acquired by groups and agents throughout their previous struggles. It particularly represents "all the power they possess over the instituted taxonomies, inscribed in minds or in objectivity" (p. 732). This power is unevenly distributed so that "[t]hose most visible in terms of the prevailing categories of perception are those best placed to change the vision by changing the categories of perception. But also, on the whole, those least inclined to do so" (p. 732).

Big media businesses who own the means of production have the greatest power to transform society, but also the least to gain from a transformation. The focus of Bourdieu's cultural sociology, and the reason that his framework is indispensible for the analysis of symbolic disruption from a spatial perspective, is the project to describe "the structures which govern both practices and the concomitant representations" (Bourdieu, 1977b, p. 21). Once again, we must always look at both what Jenkins (2006) calls social protocols *and* cultural protocols, in conjunction with each other. Bourdieu explains this further:

> This means that one cannot conduct a science of classifications without conducting a science of the struggle over classifications and without taking account of the position occupied, in this struggle over the power of knowledge, for power through knowledge, for the monopoly of legitimate symbolic violence, by each of the agents or groups of agents who are involved in it, whether they be ordinary individuals, exposed to the vicissitudes of the everyday symbolic struggle, or authorized (and fulltime) professionals. (Bourdieu, 1985, p. 734)

The bottom line here is that in order to analyze hegemony and resistance, one must take into account classifications (language/discourse/protocol) as well as the (network) position occupied by the agents and groups involved. So, while this theory of the logic of practice underlines the role of structures in explaining how the social world functions, it still allows room for disruptions: "Practice has a logic which is not that of the logician. This has to be acknowledged in order to avoid asking of it more logic than it can give, thereby condemning oneself either to wring incoherences out of it or to thrust a forced coherence upon it" (Bourdieu, 1990, p. 86).

Disruption as Rewiring

Digital culture is a complex system. As explained at the beginning of this chapter, it entails technology (mediated by protocol at the level of code) and communication (mediated by discourse at the level of language) embedded in social relations (as established via digital media). Whether we call our object of study code, protocol, discourse, or language, the place to look for it to come into being is in practice. The only way of comprehensively dealing with technological, cultural, and social aspects of the Internet without remaining in a purely philosophical domain is to empirically analyze what actually happens. Enabling and limiting structures—in the shape of protocol, discourse, and the like—must be studied in actual practice. This is a basic tenet within cultural sociology: Life in social spaces must be studied through the practice where, according to Bourdieu (1984, p. 101), habitus and capital is put into play in various fields. This practice has been described in this chapter as highly textual and thus readable.

Castells (2009, p. 412) argues that in order to enact social change in the network society, attempts must be made at "reprogramming the communications networks that constitute the symbolic environment for image manipulation and information processing in our minds, the ultimate determinants of individual and collective practices." To achieve such a rewiring, the new forms created by disruptive spaces will be crucial. But, returning to the double trap, Castells contends:

> However, the technologies of freedom are not free. Governments, parties, corporations, interest groups, churches, gangsters, and power apparatuses of every possible origin and kind have made it their priority to harness the potential of mass self-communication in the service of their specific interests. Furthermore, in spite of the diversity of these interests, there is a common goal for this variegated mob of the powers that be: to tame the liberating potential of networks of mass-self communication. They are engaged in a decisive strategic project: the electronic enclosures of our time. (2009, p. 414)

In this context, "the participatory crowds suddenly find themselves in a situation full of tension and conflict" (Lovink, 2012, p. 1). It is time to put the reality of digital grassroots politics under scrutiny: While we are in some respects standing at a new frontier of free speech, discourse may be devoid of actual transformatory power (Dean, Anderson, & Lovink, 2006). Returning to Lovink's net critical perspective, the aim now is to develop analyses of the digital by going beyond qualitative studies of the micro level as well as quantitative studies of the macro level (Lovink, 2012, p. 22).

In the next chapter I introduce the methodological approach for the case studies to follow. Connected concept analysis (CCA), a combination of existing methods aiming to bridge the qualitative/quantitative divide in text analysis, will be presented. The strategy includes quantitative elements as well as qualitative readings of texts. CCA, because it is focused on text and the production of meaning, will assume a key role in the analyses. It will be complemented with social network analysis in order to get a fuller contextualization of the interactions under study. Taken together, the approaches enable the type of "distant reading" advocated by Moretti (2005), thereby revealing shapes, relations, and structures.

· 3 ·

SHAPES, RELATIONS, STRUCTURES

*The text undergoes a process of deliberate reduction and abstraction
[. . .] where distance is however not an obstacle, but* a specific form of
knowledge: *fewer elements, hence a sharper sense of their overall interconnection. Shapes, relations, structures. Forms. Models. (Moretti,
2005, p. 1)*

The study of disruptive spaces in the rest of this book will include analyses of
social relations and of discourse, keeping in mind that discourse is in many
ways equal to social relations, and that social relations amount to discourse
(Bourdieu, 1977a). Such ambiguity is a key reason why the analysis of practice
is the most viable strategy for studying digital culture. The empirical studies in
the subsequent chapters will be based on two general forms of data analysis:
social network analysis and textual network analysis. Once again, this is keeping in mind that the social and the textual are irrevocably entangled.

I introduce in this book a specific methodological combination for text
analysis that brings several different approaches together in a new technique
for mapping semiotic processes in large datasets. I call it *connected concept*

analysis (CCA). The method combines already existing techniques from the fields of discourse analysis, network analysis, and computational linguistics in a strategy that is especially well suited for dealing with large online text datasets while still retaining a qualitative sensibility. CCA is particularly relevant to the mapping of the symbolic—discursive and linguistic—aspects, which is key to the analyses in the following chapters. I will put great emphasis upon this type of analysis because, as Bourdieu (1977a, p. 646) claims, "the social world is a system of symbolic exchanges [...] and social action is an act of communication."

In addition to CCA, social network analysis is also needed, because "[t]o give an account of discourse, we need to know the conditions governing the constitution of the group within which it functions" (Bourdieu, 1977a, p. 650). Social network methodology (Wasserman & Faust, 1994; Wellman, 1997) will be employed in some of the chapters of this book. Network visualizations based on relationships and metrics of centrality and distribution will be presented, and the analytic strategies as well as the tools used (Bastian, Heymann, & Jacomy, 2009; De Nooy, Mrvar, & Batagelj, 2011) will be discussed in relation to the data presented. Chapter 7 relies in part on a model for sentiment analysis (Thelwall, Buckley, Paltoglou, & Cai, 2010) that will be described in that chapter. Throughout, the analyses of discursive and linguistic dimensions of disruptive spaces will be approached using CCA. Since this method is somewhat new, it will be explained in detail.

Beyond Triangulation

The demarcation line, and the sometimes open conflict, between qualitative and quantitative methods persists as one of the Gordian knots of social science (Durkheim, 1895; Mises, 1960). In scholarly discourse, traces still remain of a continuing *Methodenstreit* (Swedberg, 1990). Scholars who prefer case-oriented methods argue that in-depth understandings of a smaller set of observations is crucial for understanding the complexities of reality, and those who prefer variable-oriented approaches argue that only the highly systematized analysis of larger numbers of cases can produce reliable statements about the true order of things (Herrmann & Cronqvist, 2006). Today, however, there seems to be an increasing consensus that a recommendable solution to the dilemma is to employ combinations of qualitative and quantitative methods, benefiting from their various strengths while balancing their respective weaknesses (Brady & Collier, 2004; Ragin, 2000). However, most such "mixed methods" approaches rely on rigid definitions of the two respective paradigms to be combined, and suggest frameworks based on different forms of complementarity or "triangulation" (Flick, 1992; Jensen, 2002; Jick, 1979).

The qualitative tradition is seen as the more inductively, or "abductively" (Peirce, 1932), oriented interpretive study of small numbers of observations, while the quantitative tradition is characterized by the deductively oriented statistical study of large numbers of cases. This has given rise to the common notion that qualitative research produces detailed accounts through close readings (Lentricchia & DuBois, 2003; van Looy & Baetens, 2003) of social processes, while quantitative research renders more limited but controllable and generalizable information about causal relations and regularities of the social and cultural fabric. With the rise of digital culture, the conditions surrounding the gathering of data about social processes and interaction have been dramatically altered so that vast amounts of text data, including information about network links, are registered and aggregated independently of initiatives by researchers. Digital culture is one big data-collection machinery; while studies of a specific form of interaction used to require the design and implementation of an original study from scratch, the method today is to find a slice of that type of interaction readily documented on the Internet and download and prepare relevant parts for analysis.

This strategy is illustrated by, for example, Golder and Macy (2011), who mapped people's affective states throughout the day as expressed via Twitter posts in 84 countries, using a research design that was by necessity dictated by the availability and character of the time-stamped and text-based social media data. Examples of similar studies exist in several other fields (Bruns, Burgess, Highfield, Kirchhoff & Nicolai, 2011; Khonsari, Nayeri, Fathalian, & Fathalian, 2010; Sedereviciute & Valentini, 2011; Vergeer, Hermans, & Sams, 2011), and while the (often political) issues studied are highly relevant, it is nonetheless true that these researchers confronted data that was largely already available and constituted in certain ways. This illustrates how the choices of the researcher in regards to designing the data are increasingly backgrounded in digital culture. Although the choice between a quantitative or qualitative approach—as in opting for a survey or for in-depth interviews— will continue to be relevant in some contexts, scholars increasingly face the challenge of thinking up and constructing "methods" after the fact.

With the ready availability online of complex, text-based, large-scale datasets, there is an inescapable need to come to terms with the qualitative-quantitative divide. CCA is an attempt at this. No longer can one escape into a locked position where the study of meaning-making has to rely on in-depth studies of a few cases, as this would make it very obvious that the majority of the dataset was neglected. And no longer can one hide behind claims that data in large numbers must be processed according solely to the rules and conventions of statistical inquiry, because this would make it very apparent that the data (language, communication, culture) could not be understood in all of its complexity.

Qualitative and quantitative social researchers previously could exist in boxes separated by walls of incommensurability erected by their choices in generating datasets of vastly differing characters—obscuring the inevitable co-existence of qualitative and quantitative aspects in reality. Now, facing the challenge of large online texts that lay bare the fact that meaning-making happens in large numbers, and the fact that these large numbers cannot be understood without in-depth interpretation, we must find new and creative approaches. Texts are irrevocably embedded in systems of language and culture, from which their understanding must not be disconnected (Eco, 1976; Saussure, 1960; Van Leeuwen, 2005). While texts may be quantitatively deconstructed through approaches in content analysis (Berelson, 1952; Krippendorff, 1980; Neuendorf, 2002), physics (Bernhardsson, Da Rocha, & Minnhagen, 2010; Zipf, 1935), or computational linguistics (Deerwester, Dumais, Furnas, Landauer, & Harshman, 1990; Joshi, 1991; Manning, Schütze, & MITCogNet, 1999; Woods, 1970), these methods will dissolve the data in ways that make variable-oriented strategies the only way to proceed with the analysis. CCA is an approach to language and discourse that retains the epistemology of cultural analysis (Bourdieu, 1990; Foucault, 1971) while dealing with large datasets. This is done through the application of "the constant comparative technique" (Glaser, 1965) in an analysis employing tools from bibliometrics (Osareh, 1996) and social network analysis (De Nooy et al., 2011; Wasserman & Faust, 1994) while reworking notions from discourse theory (Laclau & Mouffe, 1985).

A Qualitative Approach to Quantity

Instead of choosing between interpretive qualitative analysis of a smaller sample of text or simply counting words and doing math with the frequencies, CCA confronts the challenge of large online texts by presenting a model based on the idea of distant reading. One starts from the epistemology of close reading and works through "a process of deliberate reduction and abstraction" to end up with—once more—"fewer elements, hence a sharper sense of their overall interconnection" (Moretti, 2005, p. 1). This represents a move in text analysis past and beyond mixed methods approaches based on 1+1 combinations or triangulation. CCA is an integrated and oscillating method tying qualitative and quantitative considerations together in one unified model that results in a graphic visualization of a discourse, arrived at without sacrificing the interpretive and subjective element that is unavoidable in the study of semiosis. This following section is quite technical yet crucial to this book's attempt to analyze discursive practice from a network perspective.

To illustrate how CCA works, a dataset from an online support forum for victims of domestic violence, henceforth called DVForum, will be used. The dataset represents a six-year sample from this discussion board that was collected using the Mozenda web-scraping software. The material spans the period from February 2003 to August 2010, and includes 16,850 full-text entries from 3,800 participants to 3,300 discussion threads. These particular data are used here with the sole purpose of illustrating the method. When working with CCA, the initial question will be the classic one for inductively oriented qualitative analysis: "What is going on here?" (Glaser, 1978, p. 57)—a question clearly oriented towards practice. Of course, the researcher does not enter the process as an entirely clean slate; he or she will have various preconceptions or agendas that may range from hunches to readily formulated hypotheses for testing. Still, at this point, the objective will be to find out how the text content is thematically constituted.

Traditionally, the qualitative strategy would entail selecting a smaller sample of the 16,850 entries for close reading, hermeneutic interpretation, and subjective coding, but CCA allows us to keep all of the units in the analysis without abandoning the interpretive stance in favor of standardized variable analysis. CCA relies on the frequent oscillation between traditionally quantitative and qualitative domains. The process described below can be efficiently performed with the help of the analysis tool Textometrica (Lindgren & Palm, 2011), but all of the described operations also could be carried out using other software.

CCA moves through a series of six quantitative and qualitative analytical steps, gradually sculpting the answer to the initial question "What is going on here?" The six steps are preceded by two steps of sociocultural meaning-making that are uncontrollable by the researcher. In the case of the DVForum, users engage in a process of *semiosis* (Fairclough, 1989; Peirce, 1932) where meaning is constructed (Gergen, 1985) and communicated in relation to prevailing protocols and discourses. The communicated content is then *aggregated* as some meanings, manners of speaking, and fields of tension or conflict are rendered prominent through discursive practice (Fairclough, 1995; Foucault, 1971).

In CCA, the first step is to atomize discourse, like taking apart a large jigsaw puzzle and jumbling the pieces. The rest of the process consists of the researcher's work in putting the pieces back together again, realizing the inner architecture of the present discourse along the way. The atomization is a strictly quantitative and objective operation that can be made in just one way, and entails creating a complete inventory of all semiotic units (words) used in the mass of text under analysis. The second step represents the first qualitative measure, which aims to filter out units that are irrelevant to the analysis and clutter up the top of the word-frequency list. In terms of computational linguistics, this corresponds to applying a list of stop words, abbreviations, and symbols to be removed from the analysis. While stop words can be identified automatically as having the same likelihood of appearing in any document in the set (Wilbur & Sirotkin, 1992), this step also has a highly subjective element, because the researcher is free to include or exclude any words or symbols in the stop list according to what he or she finds relevant to the dataset at hand. In an online forum, for example, the stop list may have to include units that reoccur in the headers or footers of all entries.

The key third step of *conceptualization* has a markedly qualitative character, and builds on the constant comparative technique as described by Glaser (1965). This technique is developed for generating categories (and in the end, theory) through qualitative coding. It is an iterative process whereby the researcher works through the word frequency list from top to bottom. In the case of DVForum, the list consists of 77,243 unique word forms after the removal of stop words. The descending frequencies range from 1,040 (for the word *abuse*) down to 1 (for 47,825 different words). Starting from the top with *abuse*, the researcher will use automated text searches to look up the specific places in forum posts where the word *abuse* is used. In theory, readings may include all 1,040 locations, but in practice, the researcher will often stop at the point of "saturation" (Glaser & Strauss, 1967, p. 61)—that is, when repeated new observations no longer lead to any significant revisions of the categories. Work with each individual word will lead to one of three possible scenarios.

If the reading of these locations leaves the researcher with the impression that the individual uses of *abuse* lack any common denominator, the word will have to be added to the stop list and removed from the rest of the analysis. This is the first scenario, which will result in the researcher *extending the filter*. If, instead, the researcher finds one unifying and common context in which this word is used, these locations can all be assigned to the same category. This category can be named "abuse," or given a more descriptive title that gives more information about the discovered context. This is the second scenario, and it consists in *connecting all occurrences to one category*. If, finally, the researcher finds that the word under analysis belongs to more than one semiotic context, these must be separated from each other and categorized accordingly. If, say, *abuse* is used sometimes to refer to the occurrence of violence in close relationships, and sometimes in reference to an organization called "Stop Abuse Now," the researcher must recode the dataset so that stop_abuse_now becomes one distinct unit in the frequency list, while other uses remain tied to the word *abuse*. This is the third scenario, of *further atomization and the creation of several categories*.

The researcher will repeat this down the list, sometimes choosing to exclude words, sometimes letting words form the basis for a semiotic category, and sometimes splitting up words into more precise units and assigning these to categories. Once again, in theory this work may include all of the 77,243 words, but in practice the work will be terminated as "saturation" is reached. In accordance with the constant comparative technique, the process iteratively varies between creating, revising, deleting, splitting, and merging categories, thus gradually refining the image of the discursive practice—that is, of "what is going on." Basically, this is standard qualitative coding and conceptualization. The difference is that one is not working with raw full text starting at point zero; instead, with CCA, one is guided by information about word frequencies, leading the researcher to key places throughout a large dataset, but still allowing for qualitative interpretations of the words in context. The end product of this step of the analysis is a set of qualitative concepts connected to a number of individual words that will function as indicators of the concept in the next step.

The fourth step of *connection* is a quantitative operation based on the bibliometric technique of co-word analysis, which rests on the assumption that the co-occurrence of certain words describes the contents of full text data (Callon, Courtial, & Laville, 1991, p. 160). In CCA, this idea is applied not to the raw words presented in the initial frequency list, but to the qualitatively generated concepts from the previous step. Textometrica or similar software will divide the data into text blocks as delimited by the researcher (e.g., the individual DVForum posts in the present example), and then establish a list of unique words occurring in each of these blocks. It then performs a co-occurrence analysis based on the qualitative concepts rather than on the words alone. The output, then, is not a list of co-occurrences of words, as in co-word analysis, but a co-concept analysis that identifies co-occurrences of words that in turn indicate the qualitative concepts. The end result of this analytical step is a list of all co-occurring concepts listed by frequency; that is, by the number of text blocks in which they appear together.

This frequency list can be exported as network data that can be interpreted by software programs for network analysis such as Pajek (De Nooy et al., 2011) or Gephi (Bastian et al., 2009). A discourse can be seen as a field or space wherein a number of symbolic components, or concepts, are positioned in relation to each other. Some of these concepts are peripheral, while others are crucial and central (Laclau & Mouffe, 1985, p. 112). The discourse thus can be analyzed as a set of differential conceptual positions and relations. Network metrics describing closeness, betweenness, centrality, cohesions, clusters, and so on (Wasserman & Faust, 1994) therefore can be used to measure the character of the discursive space under analysis. This represents a dramatic departure from previous cultural and interpretative approaches to discourse, which held that meaning-making is not measurable in this sense.

The fifth step of CCA consists of the *visualization* of the connected concepts. This corresponds to the rendering of a graph illustrating the co-concepts, and can be performed with Textometrica using the open-source Graphviz add-on (Ellson, Gansner, Koutsofios, North, & Woodhull, 2002) or with virtually any other network visualization package. Figure 1, which repre-

Figure 1. Connected concepts in an online domestic violence forum.

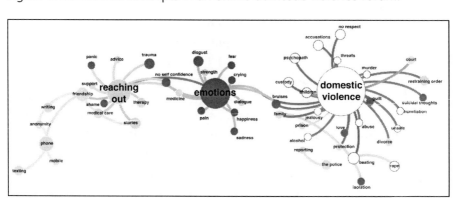

sents the connected concepts of the analysis of DVForum, was made in Gephi using the Force Atlas layout algorithm, showing only the strongest connections. The graph shows three nodal concepts that have been manually color-coded for clarity. Node sizes reflect the degree (number of connections) of each concept, and the edge color (lighter to darker) represents the number (smaller to larger) of co-occurrences between concepts. The fifth step is intertwined with the sixth step of *validation* of the analysis, as a number of considerations made when tweaking the network graph will be influenced by the qualitative familiarization with the material achieved by the researcher during the third step of the analysis. The researcher will calculate network metrics, select layout algorithms, identify clusters, and define node and edge sizes and colors in ways that best represent the relevant conceptual connections. Validation also includes the researcher looking for any anomalies or surprises in the graph, sometimes returning to step 3 to revisit language use in context and possibly revise the conceptual structure.

Towards an Analysis of Practice

As described above, the case chapters that follow are based on different methodological combinations. Mappings made with the help of social network analysis and CCA are the most prominent approaches. In light of the discussions in chapters one and two, we are interested in mapping out certain types of shapes, relations, and structures. On the social network level, we are looking for patterns of formation and mobilization: *spaces* based on a unifying social order, rather than random connections, and on commitment over time (Jones, 1997) as well as on relations of mutual accountability (Wenger, 1998); and *network disruption* through the formation of flexible, distributed networks from below that aim to circumvent the control and command of hegemonic networks (Galloway, 2004).

These themes that relate to how activist networks are formed online and with what network effects will be dealt with in chapters 4 and 5. Chapter 4 uses the case of the #WikiLeaks hashtag and poses questions regarding the possibilities for hacktivist mobilization—that is, the deployment of movements through digital tools. The chapter is focused on analysis of elusive online spaces as potential sites of mobilization. Looking at linguistic and social aspects, the main questions are: Is there a common discursive code? Is there a social order? And, is there commitment over time? Chapter 5 is based on a case study of the use of Twitter during the Libyan uprising of 2011. Focus is on the multifaceted question of who actually dominated the discourse in this medium during the uprising—activists, news organizations, or governments.

On the textual level, I map out forms of discursive unity and affinity. This is discussed in relation to several other themes: *common discursive codes*, as opposed to fragmented communication (Jones, 1997), holding spaces together through a shared repertoire for negotiating meaning (Wenger, 1998); *collaborative endeavors* rather than broader categorizations, keeping people together (Gee, 2005) in jointly negotiated enterprises (Wenger, 1998); *knowledge communities* in the form of skill zones based on the exchange of knowledge and the generation of innovation (Lévy, 1999); and *symbolic disruption* through symbolical challenges to the symbolic order (Hebdige, 1979) that obstruct the closing of the ideological circuit between sign and object (Lefebvre, 1971), interrupt the process of normalization (Barthes, 1972), challenge codes (Melucci, 1996), and resist hegemony (Gramsci, 1971). Increasing knowledge about these themes requires widening the scope to include not only political activism but also fandom, knowledge communities, enthusiast groups, support forums, discussion boards, and other settings that hold clues to understanding the dynamics of disruptive spaces. In today's complex societies, resistance and disruption come from a multitude of spaces and run in many different directions. At the same time, objectives are increasingly diverging from traditional political aims to include re-articulations, interference, and "semiotic terrorism" (Lovink, 2002, p. 313) within a range of societal spheres.

In keeping with this idea, chapter 6 is based on a case study of subtitling communities—that is, groups of fans who produce amateur subtitled versions of movies and TV series. It looks further at some issues addressed in chapters 4 and 5, but also delves deeper into the analysis of collaborative efforts to produce knowledge and informally develop skills. These themes are explored again in chapter 7, which is a case study of user-created tutorial videos on YouTube. Combining sentiment analysis (Thelwall et al., 2010) and CCA, the chapter examines the sentiments that characterize the comment discourse surrounding these videos. It also looks at the differences in comments on various types of videos, and investigates which discursive contexts seem to promote positive responses and a participatory climate.

Chapter 8 analyzes reactions to online video clips relating to school shootings. Referring to established theories about media ideology and moral panics, the chapter will discuss how online microcontent can function as noise that disrupts the discourse produced by "mainstream" or "official" outlets. For a further discussion of the border zones between pop culture disruption and "more serious matters," we turn in chapter 9 to the example of online piracy to look at how politics of the everyday—"subpolitics" (Beck, 1997) and "subactivism" (Bakardjieva, 2009)—might evolve in ways that offer clues about how social movements are formed in relation to the digital in the twenty-first century.

In the end—to synthesize the analyses—we are looking for expressions of how the struggle between hegemony and resistance plays out in digital culture: *successful tactics* for the oppositional use of emergent technologies (Garcia & Lovink, 1997; Kahn & Kellner, 2008; Raley, 2009), which involves not only things traditionally understood to be political (Carpentier, 2011), but also resistance to any form of antagonism that arises within a large number of settings (Mouffe, 2000); *counterpublic spheres* taking shape (Warner, 2002); and traces indicating the power of disruptive spaces to interconnect in "cosmopedic" (Lévy, 1999) ways to form some sort of grassroots "hive mind" (Kroski, 2005; Lanier, 2010).

· 4 ·

HACKTIVIST MOBILIZATION

(Social) space is not a thing among other things, nor a product among other products; rather, it subsumes things produced and encompasses their interrelationships in their coexistence and simultaneity—their (relative) order and/or (relative) disorder. (Lefebvre, 1974, p. 73)

Currently, a good deal of attention is focused on the role of networked digital media in political processes around the world. In particular, much discourse relates to the potential uses of new social tools and platforms by grassroots interest groups, social movements, NGOs, and oppressed populations to voice their concerns, talk back to the powers that be, and actually make a difference. A number of uprisings across the globe during the last couple of years have been popularly labeled "Twitter revolutions": the civil unrest following the 2009 elections in Moldova (Munteanu & Mungiu-Pippidi, 2009), the Iranian election protests in 2009 and 2010 (Burns & Eltham, 2009; Grossman, 2009), the 2010 to 2011 Tunisian protests against the Ben Ali regime, and the 2011 Egyptian protests against President Mubarak (Jansen, 2010). During the second part of 2011, the events of the so-called Arab Spring often were bundled together with the emergence of the Occupy movement (Gessen, 2012) and hacktivist initiatives such as Anonymous and LulzSec (Barnard-Wills, 2011) in discussions of "why it's kicking off everywhere" (Skinner, 2011; Mason, 2012).

All of these cases involve using digital tools to disturb or circumvent official flows of information from traditional media or economic and governmental institutions. Over the last few years, these processes have been highlighted also in less tumultuous political contexts. For example, Barack Obama's victory in the 2008 U.S. presidential election was commonly attributed to the mobilization of a broad grassroots movement on the Internet (Boehlert, 2009; Harfoush, 2009), and the role of digital media in democratic elections has been discussed by a number of scholars (Gibson, Römmele et al., 2003; Tolbert & McNeal, 2003; Hooghe & Teepe, 2007; Anstead & Chadwick, 2008; Vergeer, Hermans et al., 2011).

When it comes to the democratizing potential of new media, in 1947 Adorno and Horkheimer already were skeptical about the celebration of the new media of the mid-twentieth century (radio, television, and film). According to them, arguments about the liberating power of the new media had just as much to do with generating economic profit for private media corporations as with making the audience play a larger part in political processes (cf. Fuchs, 2008, 2011). For Adorno and Horkheimer (1947), "the cultural industry" not only controlled technology and content, but also contributed significantly to the shaping of opinions and consent in relation to the prevailing social institutions. Similarly, today, political mobilization, participation, and activism through social media may be obstructed at the start by the fact that big media companies and governments dominate the digital public sphere to the extent that it is impossible for the tail of individual users, however long it may be (Anderson, 2006), to form any substantial and sufficiently homogenous counterpublic sphere (Fraser, 1990; Warner, 2002b; Downey & Fenton, 2003). In addition, as discussed in chapter 1, activism through social media has been said to promote a watered-down and nonengaged "slacktivism" (Christensen, 2011; Morozov, 2011) or "clicktivism" (White, 2010), where we are mistaking low-threshold user behaviors similar to those associated with marketing campaigns for actual commitment and sacrifice.

In spite of these relevant criticisms, it is nonetheless obvious that activism now happens in other, sometimes more massive and powerful ways than it did before the coming of digital media. This chapter and the next address issues of how disruptive spaces are formed and how they operate to disrupt dominant networks of communication. As I argued in chapters 1 and 2, the question about the realization of the participatory potentials of digital media is ultimately not a philosophical or theoretical question, but an empirical one that can be explored through systematic analysis of actual practice. Since 2007, Twitter users have used so-called *hashtags*—keywords marked with the # symbol—to indicate discussion "channels" within the largely unstructured flow of posts through the service. While often used in playful ways, hashtags also have proven to be efficient for constituting "ad-hoc publics" to mobilize people in relation to significant events (Bruns & Burgess, 2011). The case studies in these two chapters are based on CCA and social network analysis of one dataset of communication employing the #WikiLeaks hashtag (chapter 4), and another of communication using the #feb17 hashtag (chapter 5) during the first twenty-four hours of protests in Libya during the Arab Spring in 2011.

The Hashtag as Settlement

The traditional image of a social movement includes meetings, rallies, and protests: activities that take place in concrete physical places, where members of the movement are brought together and synchronized in a common endeavor to change society. Digital media has started to change this image. Today, there is talk of how "movements" are formed in the digital. At the same time, the Internet is often described in terms of its conduciveness to facelessness and loose ties. Online spaces are volatile and fragmented.

This chapter looks at Twitter activity under the #WikiLeaks hashtag to analyze the potential of elusive web spaces as sites of mobilization. A total of 1,029 tweets during May and June 2010 were collected, and the data were subjected to these main questions: What are the characteristics of the communication in terms of common discursive codes versus fragmentation? In what respects can social order be distinguished, and to what extent are connections between users simply random? Are there any prominent patterns as regards the commitment of participators over time?

These questions were derived from Jones' (1997) writings on virtual settlements (see chapter 1). According to Jones, an online place where group communication takes place has to meet four basic conditions to qualify as a virtual settlement: "(1) a minimum level of interactivity; (2) a variety of communicators; (3) a virtual common-public-space where a significant portion of interactive group-CMCs occur"; and "(4) a minimum level of sustained membership" (Jones, 1997, n.p.). I will use these four criteria to address the question of whether an essentially borderless and elusive site such as the symbolic space of a Twitter hashtag can be a virtual settlement—a coherent space. How is the culture surrounding the hashtag constituted? How are participants positioned? To which fundamental patterns does its social interaction adhere?

WikiLeaks, a hacktivist project started in 2007, is an international organization that posts on its website (http://wikileaks.org) documents that would otherwise be unavailable to the public. Among the notable documents it has leaked are the 2003 standard operating procedures of the U.S. Army at the Guantánamo Bay detention camp (leaked in 2007), the contents of Sarah Palin's private Yahoo email account (leaked during the 2008 U.S. presidential campaign), 570,000 pager messages sent on the day of the 9/11 attack in 2001 (leaked in 2009), and the 2007 Baghdad airstrike video (leaked in 2010). The controversial organization, directed by the Australian journalist Julian Assange, has received a lot of attention from the news media and won several media awards. Activists connected to WikiLeaks have reported that they often have been harassed and monitored by governments, police, and intelligence agencies. The "About us" section on the WikiLeaks website states that:

> WikiLeaks is a multi-jurisdictional public service designed to protect whistleblowers, journalists and activists who have sensitive materials to communicate to the public. Since July 2007, we have worked across the globe to obtain, publish and defend such materials, and, also, to fight in the legal and political spheres for the broader principles on which our work is based: the integrity of our common historical record and the rights of all peoples to create new history.
> [...]
> WikiLeaks combines the protection and anonymity of cutting-edge cryptographic technologies with the comfortable presentation style of Wikipedia, although the two are not otherwise related. Our network also collects materials in person and from postal drops. We also run a network of lawyers and others to defend our work and our sources. WikiLeaks information is distributed across many jurisdictions, organizations and individuals. Once a document published it is essentially impossible to censor.

The WikiLeaks site is hosted by a company based in Sweden that offers "refugee hosting." The company website (http://prq.se) states that their "boundless commitment to free speech has been tested and proven over and over again. If it is legal in Sweden, we will host it, and will keep it up regardless of any pressure to take it down." According to Wikipedia, this company is owned by two of the people behind the much publicized and prosecuted file-sharing tracker The Pirate Bay.

The discussions in this chapter and the next are based on a combination of CCA, social network analysis, and an analysis of the texts of tweets. First we turn to the aspects of mobilization that have to do with language and meaning-making.

Discursive Aspects of Mobilization

A visualization of the connected concept network of tweets on #WikiLeaks is shown in Figure 2. The vertices are of various sizes that indicate how common certain concepts are, and the arrows binding them together illustrate links in terms of co-occurrences between them. Looking more closely at the figure, one

Figure 2. Connected concepts for #WikiLeaks on Twitter, May–June 2010.

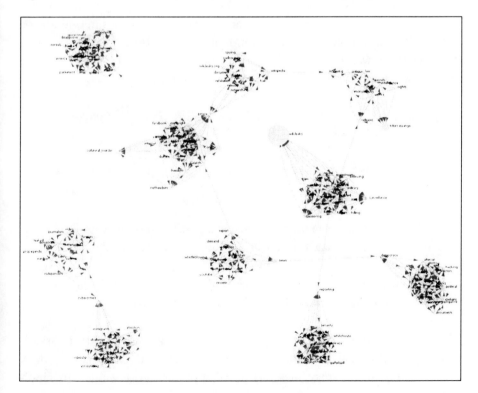

finds a number of discursive themes, or clusters, that show how tweet topics relating to WikiLeaks are ordered. Some groups of vertices (so-called clusters) are about general issues of censorship and democracy; others are about promoting WikiLeaks, asking for donations, specific leaks and their reception, and so on. Without going into detailed analysis of this, the main point is that there is indeed discursive structure, even though Twitter as a platform is completely open (apart from the 140-character limit for tweets) and does not require structure (as, for example, a discussion forum structured into threads with replies to an initial post). Figure 2 illustrates that there is a thematic structure underlying the individual tweets.

A closer reading of the actual tweet content also reveals that certain themes are more prominent than others. First of all, a very large number of tweets consisted of links to various types of news stories, primarily articles and videos produced by British and U.S. media corporations. Often formulated explicitly as reading suggestions, these posts often are retweeted extensively, making this category of posts the largest of the categories discussed here. One of the core themes, then, is the sharing and circulation of knowledge and information. The first two tweets below are examples of the frequent suggestions to read dominant media news items that appear to support WikiLeaks in one way or another. Recommendations of other kinds of texts are also quite common. The third tweet below, for example, links to a video of a European Union hearing, and the last one contains a link to a more critical text.

> Excellent read: Hail to the whistleblowers http://bit.ly/doZ5mj #wikileaks #afghanistan

> awesome ABC doco on #wikileaks interviews, details on how they protect sources & seeking world wide free press history http://bit.ly/aWsHQl

> Watch the summary of the #aldefe seminar (Self) Censorship with @marietjed66 Julian Assange #wikileaks a.o. http://youtu.be/DFSHv9coCN8

> Federation of American Scientists: #Wikileaks aren't whistleblowers, they're 'information vandals' http://tinyurl.com/252ahv9

The views and interests represented and referenced are not homogenous. Although posts that unequivocally support WikiLeaks clearly dominate the data, the number of links to texts making critical or problematizing arguments indicates that the space is not closed to other views or debate. Nevertheless, because such a large proportion of these tweets refer to discourse produced by large Western media corporations, the voiced tensions and conflicts largely reflect those produced in dominant media discourse.

Another significant group of tweets calls for various forms of direct action in support of WikiLeaks. The most common action called for is the donation of money to WikiLeaks; the first of the four tweets quoted below belongs to this particular group, and also to the category of reading suggestions. The second quote also calls for a donation, as well as sharing of the link. Sharing stories and encouraging action are often linked.

> #wikileaks #stopthewar #cowardlypredators Photo and article of one of the great heroes of our time: http://is.gd/cZ5oz—Donate today

> Support and donate to #Wikileaks http://www.countercurrents.org/assange150610.htm Share and favor the notice!

> Another way you can help #WIKILEAKS: run a Tor server http://tor-project.org/

> Sick and tired of the corruption around. Anyone willing to take the photos with me and put them online #wikileaks kenya

The last two tweets above suggest even more direct forms of action. Although such calls are less common and retweeted less frequently, it is nevertheless apparent that references to concrete, hands-on political action is also part of the discourse. A third category of tweets consists of political and philosophical slogans used to defend freedom of speech and a free press. Three examples of this are quoted below.

> 'Want a revolution? Just being able to hear the truth will change the world' #dancarlin #opengovernment #wikileaks

> The truth harms only the Liars. The lies cover up the murder of thousands of innocent civilians. #WikiLeaks #WhistleBlowers #TruthTellers

> 'Our lives begin to end the day we become silent about things that matter' MLK jr. #wikileaks #thai #government #censorship

The use of political slogans such as these not only frames the political am-
bitions of the WikiLeaks organization in positive terms, but also constructs
digital political space as a crucial arena for political action in a very broad
sense. From the perspective of these particular Twitter users, hacktivism
deals with political issues that reach far beyond strictly digital space. The
tweet categories discussed thus far relate to the articulation of common values, identities, and practices; other types of tweets construct the identity of
the political enemy. Of the following six quoted tweets, the first four articulate antagonistic relations between WikiLeaks and representatives of the na-
tion-state, and the last two suggest that large corporations are threatened by
WikiLeaks.

> #Obama cracks down on truth & justice, these elements are very bad for
> our national security?, HUH? (maybe BAD 4 Obama's image! #wikileaks

> Classic!! @wikileaks Julian Assange out-lawyers the lawyer in Euro Par-
> liament http://bit.ly/dnpM2X #wikileaks

> Australia retaliates against Wikileaks—http://bit.ly/bgbQjw intimida-
> tion much? #wikileaks #censorship

> Whistleblowers play big role in exposing crimes in #China.
> http://bit.ly/dCALwC #wikileaks #ChinaEdition

> Next #spill is #wikileaks to take out Rupert.

> @KateSherrod: A call for BP workers to step up and spill to #Wikileaks
> http://c4ss.org/content/2956

Whereas the common "we" is defined without reference to territorial, national, or ethnic relations, but rather in a global sense, it is interesting to note
that its antagonists are defined by their government or corporate identities.
Using a term from Laclau and Mouffe (1985), it could be argued that through
"chains of equivalence," government and corporate identities and interests
such as these are grouped together and articulated as having agendas that conflict with those of WikiLeaks and the globally defined common people. This
imagery is strengthened by the large number of tweets that predict a leak about
a global Internet surveillance system:

#Wikileaks founder Assange drops mass spying hint http://j.mp/banxab
abcNews #Orwell

#wikileaks supposedly Assange has uncovered vast worldwide survai-
lence & monitoring of people, oh really, what @telecomix

The next big leak will might reveal a global 1984 surveillance system ?
http://bit.ly/bF7RGr #wikileaks #freemanning

The main idea in Laclau and Mouffe's discourse theory is that connections
between meaningful elements within a discourse can be analyzed in terms of
how links between concepts are asserted and authorized, how signifiers are
grouped, and how certain arrangements cling together. Looking at concept frequencies in the data and reviewing parts of it qualitatively, the impression is
that Twitter discourse on #WikiLeaks generally tends to approve of the activities of the organization, and the necessity of its actions is presented in terms
of democracy, anticensorship, and activism.

Social Aspects of Mobilization

These dynamics can be further investigated by analyzing not only the written discourse, but also the social positioning and hierarchies of participants.
Once again: In order to be able to "give an account of discourse; we need to
know the conditions governing the constitution of the group within which
it functions" (Bourdieu, 1977a, p. 650). Jones (1997) defines a virtual settlement as "a cyber-place that is symbolically delineated by topic of interest
and within which a significant proportion of interrelated interactive group-
CMC [computer-mediated communication] occurs." This parallels Bourdieu's statement that any social field is always delineated by a doxa—a set of
fundamental rules or presuppositions that are specific to the field: "All those
who are involved in the fields [. . .] share a tacit adherence to the same doxa
which makes their competition possible and assigns its limits" (Bourdieu,
2000, p.102).

Let us look specifically at Jones' (1997, n.p.) second criteria for a virtual settlement. He states that "a variety of communicators" is a condition that is
highly intertwined with the condition of "interactivity": "Clearly if there is
only one communicator there can be no interactivity," he writes. Figure 3 il-

Figure 3. The long tail of participants.

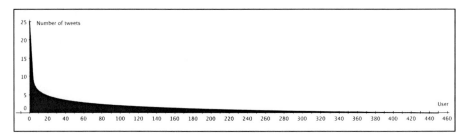

lustrates the participants (horizontal axis) listed by their numbers of tweets using the #WikiLeaks hashtag in the data from May and June 2010.

While a little more than 70% of the users have authored just one single tweet, 25% have written two to nine tweets, and a 2% core of users wrote 20% of the posts. The figure mimics the well-known long tail curve (Anderson, 2006), which relates to supply-and-demand economics. Anderson argues that in a cultural landscape where nearly everything is available, the true face of demand will reveal itself, and he predicts that the future success of business lies in catering to a large number of niche tastes. Reinterpreting this theory and applying it to the #WikiLeaks context raises the question of what the long tail represents in this setting. Does it mean that the majority of participants are uncommitted or semi-accidental supporters, or does it imply that participation might be defined as such even though it is limited to contributing only very few tweets? Liu (1999, n.p.) writes that "[a] group of 'lurkers' [noncontributing web forum users] who do not communicate cannot be called a community. For a group of individuals to qualify as a community, these individuals have to communicate and interact."

To get a grip on the practice of social interactions through the #WikiLeaks hashtag, I performed a social network analysis of relations of co-authorship. In this case, co-authorship was defined, firstly, as the relationship that is established when two users contribute to the same tweet thread via public replies to each other using the @-symbol. Secondly, retweets (confirmatory echoes of what others have tweeted, using the RT-abbreviation) were also included. The sample is once again from the May to June 2010 tweets using the #WikiLeaks hashtag (1,029 tweets by 439 users). The aim was to map and visualize the "common-public-space" established through this hashtag, and to identify basic dynamics of "interactive group-cmc" within it (Jones, 1997). Figures 4 and 5 illustrate the relations between the participants. Each vertex represents one

Figure 4. Periphery of network.

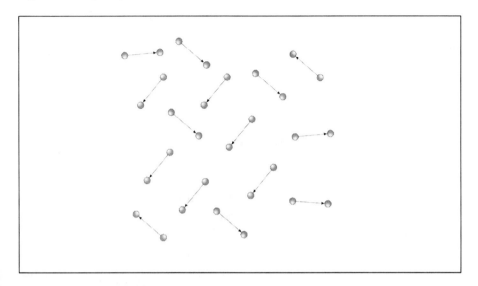

Figure 5. Center of network.

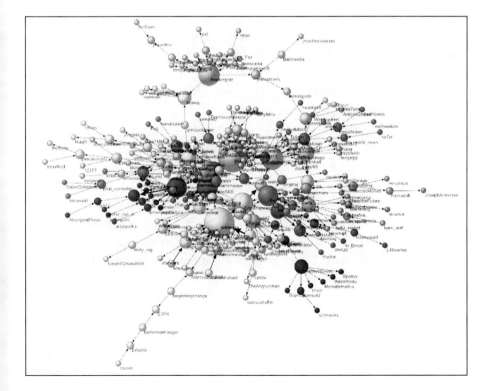

single user. Vertex size indicates the level of activity of each user (that is, how many relationships of co-authorship they are involved in), and the positions of vertices and the connections between them represent the strongest links (in terms of co-authorship) among contributors. While the peripheral regions are marked by mostly simple unidirectional and nonhierarchical connections (Figure 4), the patterns become more interesting as one moves closer to the center of the network (Figure 5).

Looking at Figure 5, it is clear that there is a relatively small number of key contributors (cf. the 5–10 largest vertices) around whom the rest of the social space is ordered. We can conclude from this that there are indeed leaders as well as followers.

As an example, let us look closer at the Twitter activities of the user freakingcat, represented by the formation of nodes at the very top of Figure 5. This subnetwork represents a series of tweets made by this user and their subsequent retweets by other users. In this particular case, all of the tweets relate to an apparent/alleged government blocking of the WikiLeaks website in Thailand, where freakingcat lives, and they were all posted on June 28 and 29. In Table 2, four tweets by freakingcat are shown in bold, followed by a selection of retweets in italics. As can be seen in this table (and also in the co-authorship analysis in Figure 5), freakingcat is retweeted by a large number of different users. Furthermore, as can be seen in the elapsed time column, most of the retweets were made within minutes of the initial post. Freakingcat, then, is a user who was able to influence speech among a large number of users fairly rapidly within this particular discursive field.

The tweets and retweets in Table 2 correspond to several of the previously discussed key categories of #WikiLeaks tweets, as well as to key moments of hacktivism and social movement formation. The posts are illustrative of an antagonistic relationship between freedom and government, and they quote anticensorship slogans to assert the political legitimacy and magnitude of the issue. Furthermore, the two final tweets and their subsequent retweets call for collective action in the form of retweeting, and for sharing links to hacktivist responses to government control via established mirror sites. This example shows how closely related these different aspects of social and political mobilization are, and how tightly linked they are to the common language and practices of the disruptive space.

Let us finally briefly consider Jones' condition that a virtual settlement must have a minimum level of sustained membership (Jones, 1997). Similarly, Erickson (1997, p. 1) writes that virtual communities can be defined as "computer-

Table 2: Tweets (Freakingcat's and Related) Using the #WikiLeaks Hashtag,
June 28–29, 2010

USER	CONTENT	ELAPSED TIME
freakingcat	Freedom of information took a heavy beating today with Thai government censoring #wikileaks.org - raises question what they want to hide?!	0.00.00
Mark_Coughlan	RT @freakingcat: Freedom of information took a heavy beating today with Thai government censoring #wikileaks.org - raises question what ...	0.02.09
freakingcat	I disapprove of what you say, but I will defend to the death your right to say it! #wikileaks #thai #government #censorship	2.52.04
FreeTheInternet	RT @freakingcat 'I disapprove of what you say, but I will defend to the death your right to say it!' #wikileaks #thai ... #FreeTheInternet	2.56.21
elgrodo	RT @freakingcat: 'I disapprove of what you say, but I will defend to the death your right to say it!' #wikileaks #thai #government #cens ...	2.57.06
freakingcat	This Twitter Petition to demand unblocking of #wikileaks will be sent every day, until hopefully somebody will listen! Please RT it!	14.06.09
hbmacale	RT @freakingcat: This Twitter Petition to demand unblocking of #wikileaks will be sent everyday, until hopefully sum1 wil listen! Please RT!	14.07.32
jonrandy	RT @freakingcat: This Twitter Petition to demand unblocking of #wikileaks will be sent every day, until hopefully somebody will listen! ...	14.11.22
freakingcat	After #thai #government blocked #wikileaks you can still access it through their mirror sites: wikileaks.info wikileaks.se nyud.net	15.24.42
Johan_Munkestam	RT @freakingcat: After #thai #government blocked #wikileaks you can still access it through their mirror sites: wikileaks.info wikileak ...	17.17.46
BangkokBill	RT @freakingcat: After #thai #government blocked #wikileaks U cn still access it thru thr mirror sites: wikileaks.info wikileaks.se nyud.net	20.07.33

mediated social interaction among large groups of people, particularly long term, textually-mediated interaction." The existence of online discourse on a topic does not necessarily mean that an actual community exists, and it is therefore relevant to evaluate the degree of participants' commitment over time.

Figure 6 is based on a larger archive of the #WikiLeaks hashtag (37,416 tweets), and the vertices in it show clusters of the most prolific users in each month from April to August 2010. Clusters are positioned in the columns corresponding to the months in which users debuted as contributors to the hashtag, and the lines between them indicate the frequency of their postings during following months. For example, while the contributors making up cluster 3 can be identified as a cohesive unit in the data in April 2010, the same cluster continued to tweet throughout May, June, July, and August. As a whole, the results of the analysis indicate that there is "a minimum level" of sustained membership on this scene. Although it is reasonable to assume that a substantial number of participants make single posts or take part in only one thread on the forum, this is certainly not a pattern that is valid for the core clusters of contributors. There are relatively substantial groups of key tweeters who stay committed to the scene.

Figure 6. Sustained contributions to the #WikiLeaks hashtag, April–August
2010 (n=37,416).

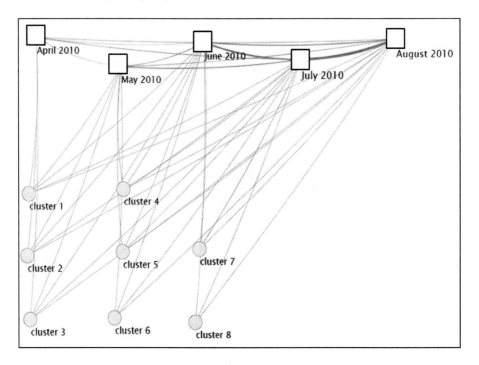

Semiotic Dynamics

This example has demonstrated that the social and the spatial always are interlinked, as space is constantly structured by those who occupy it and by how
they appropriate it (Lefebvre, 1974; Bourdieu, 1990). Space is always a social
product marked by various spatial practices that can be read and interpreted.
In this chapter I analyzed the potential of elusive and fluid web spaces as sites
of mobilization and resistance. I used the case of the #WikiLeaks hashtag on
Twitter, and looked at the cultural and social protocols governing this hacktivist space. This entailed an analysis of the discourse as well as the social exchange that is taking place. In order to assess the potential of this hashtag as
a site of mobilization, I posed questions regarding the existence of a common
discursive code, social order, and commitment.

The analysis of discourse showed that the flow of tweets under the #Wiki-
Leaks hashtag is by no means an expression of random or fragmented communication. There is a general discourse in relation to which utterances are made.

Tweeters who choose to use the #WikiLeaks hashtag to indicate the "linguistic field" (Bourdieu, 1977a, p. 647) within the bounds of which their speech act is to be understood are not explicitly coordinated in any way. Rather, each user is seemingly free to decide on the tweet's content. Yet, in spite of Twitter's apparently anarchistic mode of operation, an expected type of utterance evolves and, at the aggregated level, leads to tweeting patterns that give rise to a terminology shared to some extent by anyone entering the field.

This terminology is the result of an interactive and constructive process of what might be called "semiotic dynamics." It refers to "how populations of humans or agents can establish and share semiotic systems, typically driven by their use in communication" (Cattuto, Loreto et al., 2007, p. 1461). This is similar to what can be observed in traditional human languages, where, for example, naming conventions and the employment of neologisms crystallize over time. Furthermore, the social network analyses show that this discursive structure is paired with a social structure in which there are leaders as well as followers. In this sense, the space of Twitter relations shown in Figure 5 is an illustration of what Bourdieu (1977a) means when he says that social structure can be conceived of as relations of symbolic power, and that the "linguistic competence" of a speaker is impossible to separate from his or her position in the social structure.

From the perspective of social movement theories, the emergence of this discourse and its materiality might be seen as part of the elaboration of the "cognitive praxis" (Eyerman & Jamison, 1991) of this branch of hacktivism. In order to organize and mobilize, participants need to speak a common language, agree on the definition of the situation, and formulate a shared vision. Even though it is global and loosely knit, the linguistic space of Twitter discourse is a space where such processes of meaning-production and organization might take place. In other words, the #WikiLeaks hashtag certainly can be perceived as a site of resistance and mobilization, in spite of its seemingly open, fluid, and anarchistic modality. This case study is one example of how grassroots politics, resistance, and corporate media criticism can play out in digital media, but as Henry Jenkins (2006, p. 246) writes about convergence culture, we are still "testing the waters and mapping directions." There is definitely a need for more practical knowledge of the "dynamics of these cooperation systems" (Rheingold, 2002, p. 202). In the next chapter we explore how "settlements" such as the one analyzed in this chapter interact with other spatialities (e.g., those established by governments, media corporations, organizations, etc.) in dynamic network relations of power.

· 5 ·

NETWORK POLITICS

[C]ontemporary political dynamics are decidedly different from those in previous decades: there exists today a fearful new symmetry of networks fighting networks. One must understand how networks act politically, both as rogue swarms and as mainframe grids. (Galloway & Thacker, 2007, p. 15)

As discussed in chapter 2, the structure of any social field can be conceived of in terms of relations of symbolic power. This is—we remember—because "the social world is a system of symbolic exchanges," and "social action is an act of communication" (Bourdieu, 1977a, p. 646). In the last chapter we demonstrated that the ad hoc space of a hashtag can indeed function as a space of mobilization and disruption. But any social space is also involved in the multidimensional space of society, where different spaces are "more or less strongly and directly subordinated" to others in relations of power (Bourdieu, 1985, p. 736).

The "social reality" [. . .] is an ensemble of invisible relations, those very relations which constitute a space of positions external to each other and defined by their proximity to, neighborhood with, or distance from each other, and also by their relative position, above or below or yet in between, in the middle. (Bourdieu, 1989, p. 19)

This is another way of stating, as Galloway (2004, p. 245) does, that "network architecture is politics." This goes not only for hardware or software architecture, but also for the architecture of the social as regulated through discourse. This chapter continues where chapter 4 left off, with a closer analysis of how "settlements" or spaces interact with each other in the game where "the powers that be and the subjects of counter-power projects operate [...] in a new technological framework" (Castells, 2007, p. 239). For this, I analyze Twitter activity during the first twenty-four hours of the Libyan uprising on February 17, 2011.

The dataset consists of all Twitter replies (directed public communication between users) employing the #feb17 hashtag on February 17. Protests had begun in Libya on February 15, when a large demonstration took place in the evening outside police headquarters in Benghazi following the arrest of the human rights activist Fathi Terbil. But February 17 had been chosen by organizers on the Internet at the beginning of the month as a "Day of Revolt" for all groups opposed to Gaddafi both inside Libya and in exile. As it happened, February 17 was the first day of a month of daily protests and violent clashes until the international military intervention began on March 19, 2011.

After tweets without an addressee as well as pure retweets were filtered away, the dataset included 1,897 tweets. In order to perform a social network analysis of these data, Textometrica (Lindgren & Palm, 2011) was used to identify connections between users, and Gephi (Bastian, Heymann, & Jacomy, 2009) was used to produce the network graph shown in Figure 7. This shows the entire network of directed tweets using the #feb17 hashtag. The node sizes reflect how often a user is mentioned or replied to by any other user. Two key clusters were identified (denoted in the graph by different shades of gray). The first cluster (in the darker shade) includes the actors listed in Table 3.

The network metric of "degree," indicated in the table, is a measure of centrality that reflects the number of ties that a node has. In other terms, the degree reflects the risk of a node being part of whatever flows through the network. In this particular case, the degree can be interpreted as the level of relative involvement in the discourse taking place in the ad hoc public forming under the #feb17 hashtag. Generally, this cluster can be defined as an activist cluster because it comprises two activist organizations and three individual activists. At its periphery is the Twitter account of the pan-Arabist

Figure 7. Social network graph of replies and mentions under the #feb17 hashtag.

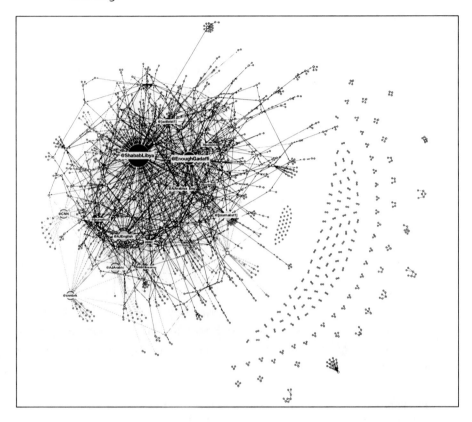

Table 3: Overview of Nodes in the Activist Cluster

Account	Degree	Type	Country/Language
@ShababLibya	130	Activist organization	Libya/English
@EnoughGaddafi	72	Activist organization	USA/English
@[activist1]*	37	Individual activist, citizen journalist	Libya/English
@[activist2]*	31	Individual activist	USA/English
@[activist3]*	20	Individual activist	USA/English
@AlArabiya_Eng	11	TV news channel	UAE/English

* Anonymized account

television news network Al Arabiya. The two organizations are Shabab Libya
and Enough Gaddafi. Shabab Libya, or the Libyan Youth Movement, describes
itself thus:

> The Libyan Youth Movement was set up during the Jan 25 Egyptian
> Revolution, it's goal, to unite the Libyan Youth both inside and out of
> Libya in preparation for the February 17 uprising. Anticipating the
> media and communication blackout in Libya we quickly set up a data-
> base of contacts across the country so as to pass information from the
> ground in real time. We are now establishing a link with the Libyan
> Transitional Council in order to support the values we believe in as well
> as ensuring the voice of Libya's youth is heard. We do not belong to a
> political party, nor to any factions. We do not receive any financial back-
> ing. The Libyan Youth Movement is currently set up in a few countries
> across the world, if you would like to get involved please get in contact
> with us. (www.shabablibya.com/about)

This is an organization working both inside and outside Libya, with a specific
focus on the day of uprising planned for February 17. In anticipation of a media
blackout, the organization works with the explicit aim of transmitting information "from the ground in real time." The other organization, Enough
Gaddafi, is based in the United States.

> Enough is born from a single, broad sentiment: the recognition of the
> overwhelming need for change in Libya. Initiated by a group of second-
> generation Libyan exiles in the United States, Enough aims to engage
> all those who share this sentiment towards the betterment of Libya.
> (www.enoughgaddafi.com)

In addition to these two organizations, the cluster includes three individual
activists who have prominent places in the discourse. The first activist, [ac-
tivist1], claims to be a pro-democracy freedom fighter based in Tripoli working
against tyranny and dictatorship. The Twitter account is linked to a Facebook
page of the same name, where the person in question states his/her ambition
of covering news from the Libyan revolution, and expresses support for Shabab
Libya. The second activist, [activist2], provides no clear personal information
in the Twitter profile, but from his/her tweet content, followers, accounts followed, and lists created, [activist2] seems to be highly active in a field very

Table 4: Overview of Nodes in the News Corporation Cluster

Account	Degree	Type	Country/Language
@AJEnglish	61	TV news channel	Quatar/English
@[journalist1]*	41	TV news journalist/activist	Venezuela/Multi-Lingual
@AJArabic	27	TV news channel	Quatar/Arabic
@CNN	21	TV news channel	USA/English
@cnnbrk	21	TV news channel	USA/English
@[journalist2]*	16	TV news journalist	USA/English
@BBC	14	TV news channel	UK/English
@BBCBreaking	13	TV news channel	UK/English

* Anonymized account

similar to [activist1]'s. Although [activist2] provides no location data, network relations and language fluency suggest that he/she is a U.S.-based Libyan exile. The third activist, [activist3], is a U.S.-based artist of Libyan descent who has an active presence on several social platforms on the Internet, and combines the promotion of performances and recordings with political messages relating to the uprising in Libya.

The second key grouping, shown in Table 4, can be defined as a news corporation cluster because all eight of its Twitter accounts are related to major news corporations. Two of the accounts are connected to CNN, and thus U.S.-based; two are British and belong to the BBC; two belong to Al Jazeera, which is located in Qatar; and the final two are owned by two individual journalists. These journalists work for two of the news corporations included in the cluster, and one of them is particularly active on Twitter in a way that moves beyond journalism and into the realm of activism.

The Power of Directionality

Summing up the analysis of these two clusters, communication under the #feb17 hashtag appears to be centered on fourteen Twitter accounts that account for a relatively substantial number of inward and outward tweets. Nearly all of this communication is in English. The core accounts are in turn interconnected in two key clusters, and although there are some overlaps, we can differentiate an activist cluster and a news corporation cluster. Looking at the degree metric, the activist cluster and the news corporation cluster have total degrees of 301 and 214, respectively. While this indicates that the activist cluster is more influential than the news corporation cluster in terms of network flow, one must keep in mind that the sum total of network flow (degree) is 3,586; this means that the two prominent clusters absorb and represent no more than 14% of all communication in the network. What is also striking is that the nodes in the two key clusters are the Twitter accounts of traditional media companies and their journalists, plus a small number of activist organizations and especially high-profile activists. What we do not see are any obvious traces of grassroots mobilization. Nor are there any government actors from any country present in the network core.

One way of exploring the remaining 86% of network flow is to apply the bow-tie theory of the web to the graph presented in Figure 7 (Barabási, 2002, p. 166; Broder et al., 2000). According to this theory, directed networks—such as links between websites, or the Twitter network under analysis in this chapter—break down naturally into a set of well-defined parts, or "continents." In the central core, each node is linked to every other node in the sense that each node can be reached from any other node. Mimicking the rough image of a bow-tie, the central core is flanked by an "in-continent" on the one hand and an "out-continent" on the other. Nodes in the in-continent are arranged so that following their links will eventually lead you to the core of the network. All nodes in the out-continent can be reached by following links from the core, but once they have been reached, there are no links returning to the center. These concepts are useful for determining where the action really is in the Twitter discourse under study. If we look only at the network metric of degree, it seems that the #feb17 discourse is dominated mainly by news corporations and a small number of activists and activist organizations, most of which are located far away from the action of the revolution. But what happens if we consider the direction of communication?

By using Gephi to disentangle Figure 7 a more schematic visualization of the same discursive space can be achieved. Examining the network metrics of in-degree and out-degree rather than just degree (which obscures directionality), and looking up the Twitter profiles of key accounts in the respective continents, uncovered the patterns illustrated in Figure 8. Accounts were sorted into the continents based on the relationship between their in- and out-degrees. The in-degree of each node was divided by the total degree of that same node to achieve a measure of how much of the traffic at each specific Twitter account derived from incoming tweets. Accounts with a value of 0.75

Figure 8. User groups divided into the continents of the directed network.

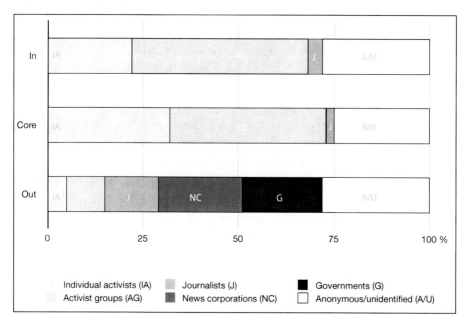

or more were seen as belonging to the out-continent, because these are ac-counts that mainly receive messages. Accounts with a value of 0.25 or less were sorted into the in-continent, because they are mainly sending messages. All other accounts (0.26–0.74) were defined as belonging to the central core because they have a balance between sending and receiving messages.

As Figure 8 shows, a categorization of Twitter accounts in terms of user type was made. The first category, labeled Individual activists (IA), includes Twitter accounts belonging to individuals rather than organizations. Accounts affili-ated with political NGOs were categorized as Activist groups (AG), and ac-counts with profiles that clearly stated that their owners are journalists were categorized as Journalists (J). Official accounts of news corporations were la-beled (NC) and governmental accounts—these were exclusively European or North American—were categorized as (G). Because this process was via a combination of manual and automated searches in lists of scraped profile data, and because most accounts on Twitter are not verified, the categorization is not exact. In fact, a relatively large number of the accounts had to be coded as Anonymous/unidentified (A/U). Still, from a qualitative standpoint, the cat-egorization aids in discerning some important differences between user types as regards the network continents to which they belong.

Firstly, governments and news organizations are to be found in the out continent. This means that they are tweeted to and about. They are mentioned as topics for discussion, and they receive criticisms and calls for attention and help. They rarely, if ever, actively take part in the exchanges that contribute to keeping the center core of the network together. A similar pattern exists for the journalist accounts, although some journalists are also active in the in continent and core. Secondly, activists and activist groups dominate the in continent as well as the central core. They are feeding information into the network by mentioning and replying to other participants. These actors appear to be engaged in relationships based on giving and/or mutuality.

The main conclusion to be drawn from Figure 8 is that while some traditional actors appear at the center of a map based solely on degree, the actual agents and actors in the network come into view if we consider the direction of communication. In the particular case of the #feb17 hashtag, a mapping based only on how much network flow passes through a given node, regardless of direction, gives the impression that the discourse is dominated by media corporations, a small number of NGOs, and particularly prominent individual activists—largely from outside of Libya. If, however, the basic network metrics of in- and out-degree are used to bring the directionality of the communicative relationships into view, a different landscape is revealed, where the share of North African accounts and tweets in Arabic seems to be significantly larger. Furthermore, accounts that were positioned at the periphery by the layout algorithm applied in Figure 7 now appear as key agents, and accounts that were at the center of that same graph are revealed to be quite passive. The operation is trivial from the perspective of network analysis, but the differences in possible interpretations of Figure 7 vis-à-vis Figure 8 are quite striking. The first way of visualizing the network suggests that grassroots mobilization is a marginal phenomenon in so-called Twitter revolutions, and could be used to argue that the communicative climate is repressive, while the second approach supports a view of individual activists and activist organizations as the prime movers of Twitter discourse. and could be used as evidence that emancipatory processes are at work.

Oh Media! Where Are You?

In Internet activism, network structures are interwoven with their discursive content (Hands, 2011, p. 91). Therefore, it is important to look not only at who says something, and to whom, but also at what is actually said. In order to explore this dimension, the content of tweets in the dataset were analyzed through connected concept analysis using Textometrica (Lindgren & Palm, 2011). The result was visualized using Gephi. As Figure 9 shows, "Al Jazeera" is the most commonly used concept in the material. It links to conceptual groups referring to "US Media," "UK Media," and "Al Arabiya" in a discursive context revolving around key concepts such as "corruption," "lies," "truth," "silenced," "oppression," "propaganda," and "false information." The mid-left section of Figure 9 illustrates the existence of a prominent theme about the struggle to achieve objective reporting and to turn the eyes of the outside world to the events in Libya. Tweets such as the following are examples of this discourse category, labeled in Figure 9 as "Calling out":

> @AJEnglish Protesters chanting, "Oh Media! Where are you? Where are you?" can barely hold back the tears as I write ... #Feb17

Figure 9. Discursive themes employed using the #feb17 hashtag.

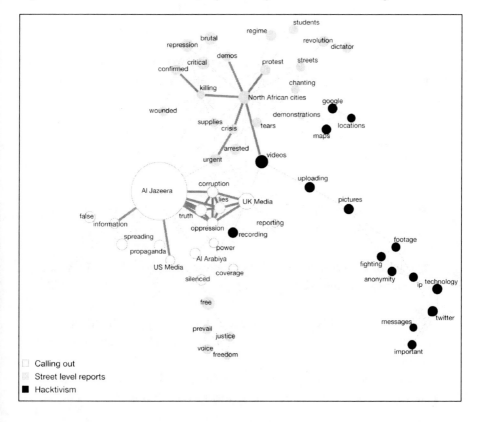

@AJEnglish covering Libya right now, THANK YOU! #Feb17 #Libya #Benghazi

@LibyaDemocracy: #FEB17 ALL CAMERAS BANNED IN #LIBYA ! MEDIA WE NEED YOU!PEOPLE ARE BEING SLAUGHTERED!

@BBCWorld http://bbc.in/gyZFLF is currently reporting about #libya .. please keep it up! #feb17

@AJArabic @AJEnglish @jrug #Libya #Feb17 PLS SHOW THIS URGENT

URGENT!! @BBCWorld @cnnbrk @ajtalk @UN NEED THE WORLD TO SEE THE CRIMES GADDAFI IS COMMITTING TODAY! #libya #feb17

The top-mid section of the graph depicts another prominent theme in the #feb17 discourse: an aggregation of concepts relating to street-level reports. Names of cities are mentioned in conjunction with "demonstrations," "streets," "students," "chanting," "wounded," "arrested," "tears," "supplies," etc. These tweets are typically about giving a live account of what is happening in demonstrations and coordinating activities as they happen. The following tweets are examples of this:

@ShababLibya: #Benghazi your city is calling you, Take to the streets. head for Maydan al Shajara #Feb17 #Libya

@ShababLibya: contact in benghazi: the city is upside down, all shops closed #Sidibouzid #Jan25 #Feb17 #Libya

@[. . .]: Downtown #Benghazi NOW! Protesters being shot at in front of the Nasr soccer club! #Libya #Feb17

@Number10gov URGENT! Shortage of medical supplies in Al Bayda hospital, calling on ALL int'l health organizations to help #Libya #Feb17

@[. . .]: #libya is revolting. we're organizing a protest at the downtown library, 1pm on saturday. come out. #feb17 #gaddafi is goin down

Finally, the mid-to-bottom right section illustrates a group of concepts relating to hacktivist activities. This conceptual subnetwork is connected to both the street-level theme and the "calling out" theme, and it revolves around the promotion and actual use of digital media to document and broadcast the rebellion. The importance of taking "pictures" and "videos" and of "uploading" them to social media platforms is underlined in these tweets:

@EnoughGaddafi: visit this site http://www.libyafeb17.com to post videos and documents related to the uprising #Feb17 #Libya

@[...]: use http://bambuser.com/ Live video streaming from your mobile phone or webcam

@[...]: try to include a hash-tag with your post, for example #Libya or #Feb17

@ShababLibya: Eyewitness on the ground: a local of #Benghazi just been killed! SPREAD THE WORD PPL WE NEED YOUR HELP #Libya #Feb17

@[...]: PLEASE ERASE ANY AND ALL INFO FROM YOUR PHONES (INCLUDING PICS & VIDEOS) AS THEY WILL BE CHECKED AT CHECKPOINTS #FEB17 #BAHRAIN

@[...]: Do NOT erase Video's and Photo's. Save them to memory card and hide memory card on your person #feb17 #Bahrain

@enoughgaddafi website hacked. Everyone change up your passwords they're bringing it hard. #libya #feb17 #Benghazi

In sum, three main themes make up the discursive field of #feb17: "Calling out," "Street-level reports," and "Hacktivism." Looking at the centrality of these respective themes, "Calling out" stands for 29% of the network flow, while "Street-level reports" and "Hacktivism" correspond to 37% and 32%, respectively. This means that the amount of discussion devoted to these subjects is close to equally distributed. These practices are examples of attempts at symbolic disruptions (Hebdige, 1979), because they aim to obstruct the closing of the ideological circuit in which traditional media institutions are a central component. The calls for attention, though directed at governments and corporate media institutions, successfully or not, constitute a backchannel to the processes of meaning production that are going on in contexts where political and media institutions are in control. Naming the acts of dictatorship "crime" and "slaughter" rather than rebukes of civil unrest is one way of going beyond the hegemonic codes. Similarly, the attempts at coordination and mobilization through technology also represent circumventions of hegemonic channels. These flows of discourse constitute an arena for expressing alternative suggestions for how the reality of social relations should be interpreted. Melucci (1996, p. 357) writes that collective action in the digital age is characterized by this type of symbolic challenge:

> The movements have waged a critical struggle against the representation of the world served up by the dominant models, denying their claim to uniqueness and challenging the symbolic constitution of politics and culture; they have refused the predominant communicative codes and they have replaced them with sounds, idioms, recognition signals that break the language of technical rationality.

What Is a Revolution?

Looking for activism under the #feb17 hashtag, I found two key clusters of users included in the Twitter discourse on the events in Libya. The activist cluster and the news corporation clusters were of similar strength, and together represented just 14% of all network flow. Focusing then on the directionality of the network, including all users, I found that activists seem to function as driving forces, while governments and news corporations achieve their prominent roles in the communication network mainly by *receiving* calls for attention from activists, citizen journalists, and other individuals or groups. This leads us to the conclusion that social media such as Twitter may in fact function as alternative media platforms where a voice other than those of the corporate media and prevailing regimes dominates. In Libya on February 17, 2011, Twitter was a field where the shots were called by activists, at least in terms of directed communication, and not counting newsflash-type tweets from major news outlets.

Turning to the actual content of the communication, another conclusion one can draw is that the activist-controlled discourse was about the above-mentioned strategy of calling out to the outside world, about coordinating demonstrations and operations at the street level, and about managing the process of digital hacktivism. But while these two conclusions show that activists make efficient use of social media in support of demonstrations and uprisings, does this also mean that "social media revolutions" are possible? In the words of Malcolm X:

> First, what is a revolution? Sometimes I'm inclined to believe that many of our people are using this word "revolution" loosely, without taking careful consideration of what this word actually means, and what its historic characteristics are. When you study the historic nature of revolutions, the motive of a revolution, the objective of a revolution, you may change words. (Malcolm X, 1963/2006, p. 21)

Revolutions are always historically embedded, and spring from frictions at the level of people's everyday lives. When revolutions come about, they tend to be seen as "the inevitable outcome of powerful social forces" (Kuran, 1989, p. 42); how powerful a force can social media constitute? In 1919, North Africa saw simultaneous uprisings in Tunisia, Egypt, and Libya in the aftermath of World War I. Those events demonstrate that Facebook, Twitter, and the Internet are not required for the global diffusion of information and expectations in a revolution. Indeed, the 1919 uprisings were inspired by Woodrow Wilson's "Fourteen Points" speech, which made its way across the globe by telegraph (Anderson, 2011). While activists in 2011 clearly used social media to share ideas and develop tactics, historically rooted cleavages and agencies are needed for technologies and aspirations to resonate in a true revolution. Why revolutions come about is a wide-stretching field of inquiry for historians, sociologists, economists, and political scientists. Social media revolutions, however, do not "come about." Social media are tools for coordinating networked publics, and they are fairly new. This means that although the present-day study of revolutions and uprisings requires expertise from the field of Internet research, the central question will never be whether social media created the revolutions in the first place.

Controlling the Flow

As we witness a transformation of the media landscape wherein empowerment of the masses is said to be a vital feature, it is important to examine whether and under what conditions the potential of this new audience position is realized. As shown in this and the previous chapter, digital social media have great potential. They can be used to effectively build relatively strong communities that are unified by common ideas, to coordinate protests and disruptive activities online as well as offline, and in a multitude of other ways to contribute to balancing existing power structures that are based on control over flows of information. However, this potential is not necessarily realized.

First, not everyone has equal access to the tools and platforms in question. Mastering them to unleash the full power of new participatory media requires certain media literacies that can be developed only if certain resources are at hand. Second, under certain conditions, the specific characteristics of digital communication may lead to disinhibition and radicalization that may hinder the process of democratization. Third, there is a tendency toward over-celebration of the liberating power of new media tools in public debate, and it is vital to evaluate such discourse in relation to concrete studies of how the tools are actually used, by whom, and to what effect. Taken together, these issues raise some questions about what types of groups most efficiently grasp the new possibilities, how democratic those groups really are, and how they are symbolically constructed and understood in the wider discursive context of the public sphere.

Even in light of the activist currents mapped in the case study presented in this chapter, it is not clear how powerful their attempts at disruption really are. What we see in these tweets is evidence that oppositional statements are being made. This indicates that social media such as Twitter may indeed be used to deploy disruption. But we need to remember the patterns in Figure 7 that show that the calls for attention are directed mostly toward the powerful, corporately controlled news media nodes. Furthermore, the attempts to challenge the symbolic representation of reality may have some impact by spreading throughout a long tail (Anderson, 2006) of users, but a question we must carry forward into the next chapters is whether a long tail, through aggregation, can add up to a substantial counterpublic (Habermas, 1989; Warner, 2002b). The activist organizations (cf. Figure 7) might function as mediators in this polarized context.

· 6 ·

*.SUB CULTURE

What the observer or the participant himself [. . .] divides into two inter-mingling trends may in reality be only one. (Simmel, 1908, p. 79)

This chapter widens the scope of the discussion by venturing into domains of "the political" (Mouffe, 2000) other than hacktivism. To fully grasp the complexities of disruptive spaces we must, as argued in chapter 3, look at a wider variety of mobilizations and creativities. Online groups that diverge from the aims of the traditional political sphere, focusing instead on symbolic politics of popular culture, may deploy skills that are relevant in a more general sense. Jenkins (2006, p. 257) writes: "The political effects [. . .] come not simply through the production and circulation of new ideas (the critical reading of [. . .] texts) but also through access to new social structures (collective intelligence) and new models of cultural production (participatory culture)."

Because of this, we turn now to the study of practice in the part of the online piracy community that is focused on the creation and distribution of subtitle files. This scene, which has its origins in the rise in online piracy of copyrighted tv and movie content in recent years, supplies subtitles to accompany ripped video files that are downloaded by users who do not speak the languages of the downloaded movies. In practice, this usually means subtitles that translate U.K. or U.S. English dialogue into languages of Europe, Asia, South America, and Africa, but sometimes also in the other direction, for example, from Japanese or Swedish into English. Online practices for distributing these subtitle files, or "subs," are similar to those for supplying scanned cover art for cds or dvds, patches, cracks, serial numbers or key generators for pirated games or other software, and free passwords for commercial sites. Additional tools that are necessary to fully benefit from pirate culture are supplied.

Setting the Subscene

Subs are plain text files containing captions that are tagged with data on frame rate, time stamps for individual lines of dialogue, and information about text formatting. The two most common file extensions are *.sub (MicroDVD format) and *.srt (SubRip format). Subtitle files are supported by a number of media player applications that overlay the text in the caption file on the displayed video content. Files distributed on the subscene are sometimes ripped in their original form straight from commercial dvds. In these cases, the captions up- and downloaded are those created by professional subtitlers for film companies. But in many other cases, what is offered are amateur translations of initially ripped subtitles, or subtitle files that are created from scratch by enthusiasts translating the dialogue by themselves and then synching the text data with the video file (these are sometimes called "fansubs"). As various versions of videos with varying frame rates circulate on pirate sites, there is sometimes a need to re-sync subtitle files, or in other ways edit or correct them, in order for them to function in new contexts.

The online subtitling community (or "subscene"), then, revolves around several forms of knowledge and expertise relating to language, movie file editing, file distribution, and site promotion. Subscene participants may therefore represent a new form of media audience betwixt and between old and new media logics, and empowered by new technologies (Jenkins, 2006, p. 24). Its dual relation, to pirate culture on the one hand and to language and interpretation on the other, makes it especially interesting to examine as a potentially disruptive space.

One way of understanding the subscene is from the perspective of democratized innovation (Herz, 2002; von Hippel, 2005) and peer production

(Benkler, 2006) to illustrate how individual hobbyists and "colonies of enthusiasts" (Rheingold, 1994, p. xxi) design and create new things with the
tools supplied by digital technologies. The Internet is sometimes said to enable dynamic forms of group-based cooperation in which "thousands of volunteers" (Benkler, 2006, p. 59) are engaged in developing technologies and
reshaping culture.

If one is to use the conceptualization put forth by Castells (2001, pp. 36–
61), the subscene cuts across several layers of "the culture of the Internet." In
this context, one would expect to meet "virtual communitarians" giving rise
to forms of online social organization characterized by "horizontal, free communication" (Castells, 2001, p. 54), as well as "hackers" with a common need
for openness and sharing and "entrepreneurs" who are forerunners in a transformation process toward a new economy marked by new rules of production,
calculation, and circulation. For the purpose of this chapter, this hybrid context will be used as the empirical basis for gaining insights into potential conflicts arising within emerging networked publics. Any space of this kind
potentially represents a site of struggle and negotiation between different
forms of power. These conflicts may promote as well as hinder the processes of
peer production (Benkler, 2006).

The analyses that follow are based on the text content of 17,582 forum
posts collected using a web-scraping application (Web Info Extractor). The
posts come from three different forums: d-addicts.com (4,216 posts), sub-
scene.com (10,447 posts), and opensubtitles.org (2,919 posts). D-addicts is
a site for sharing Asian television drama series that also hosts a large subtitling community; subscene.com and opensubtitles.org are dedicated sites for
uploading and downloading ripped and/or translated subtitles for films and
tv series.

Coordination, Collaboration, Regulation

Figure 10 is a visualization of an application of CCA to the written discourse
of the subscene. The sizes of the vertices in the graph indicate how common
certain identified themes are, and the lines illustrate the strongest links in
terms of co-occurrences between themes within posts. It appears that queries
and help, language issues, and discussions of various movie genres are the three
key nodes in subscene discourse. Discussions within the first category (queries
and help) involve the exchange of technical support for peer-to-peer sharing

Figure 10. The linguistic space of subscene.com, opensubtitles.org, and d-
    addicts.

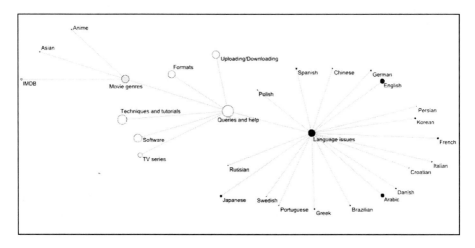

of subtitle files, and the use of different file formats. They also concern the uses
of various software and techniques to rip and/or translate the subtitles and
content of the TV series and movies that are subtitled.

Extract #1 below illustrates the fact that the subscene bears the marks of a
knowledge community where competences are pooled, traded, and exchanged
(Lévy, 1999). In this case, the first poster needs help using Korean subtitles in
the open-source media player VLC. Three community participants suggest
various solutions (changing the media player settings, downloading a special
font package, and using an alternative media player). Similar patterns are
found over and over again in the data. People's willingness to help each other
out with common technological problems, while perhaps unsurprising, is an
example of how the expertise of individual volunteers can be harnessed online
to further shared objectives and interests.

Extract #1

Hi. When I try to watch a movie with Korean subtitles using the VLC
Player, the subtitles appear distorted. For example, instead of Korean al-
phabets, strange "squares" and symbols appear instead. I searched online
relentlessly, but have found no resolution. If anyone could help, I would
REALLY APPRECIATE it. Many thanks in advance! P.S. I have Windows Vista Home Premium

VLC "Tools /Preferences / Subtitles & oSD / Default encoding" set to KOREAN. Set the Font to a font that can display Korean characters. You should find the fonts in c:\windows\fonts. That *should* work.

If you're using VLC player, download the Korean font package file, baek-muk-ttf-2.1.tar.gz" from ftp://ftp.mizi.com/pub/baekmuk/ then extract it to your \windows\fonts directory. In VLC, go to Settings>Preferences>Video>Subtitles/OSD>Text Renderer. In the font box, click browse and select the \windows\fonts directory. DON'T click on the font you want. TYPE the name. For Korean, it's usually "gulim.ttf" or "batang.ttf." Be sure not to use the "ttc" Windows OS version of the fonts since I wasn't able to get them to display the subtitles properly. Save the changes, exit the program and restart it. Now, you should be able to display Korean subtitles files in your vlc player with your movies." Don't forget to restart VLC after you've made any changes . . . just in case.

Some people say that GOMPlayerworks fine with Korean subtitles. Since they are Korea based that sounds quite likely. Good player, too. Oor you could use any player together with vobsub/vsfilter.

The subscene is an example of an emergent knowledge culture that demonstrates the ability of virtual communities to "leverage the combined expertise of their members" (Jenkins, 2006, p. 27). Its use of open-source software and the patterns of peer-to-peer sharing and support exemplify Lévy's idea that the ways in which commodity culture operates can gradually become altered by new types of audiences. The idea that help is expected to be reciprocated is illustrated in extract #2 below: The initial poster gets help in processing a file, and is reminded to upload the finished result for the community to have access to it. Extract #3 shows how the volunteer work of the subtitling community is organized and coordinated in order to provide results as efficiently as possible, and extract #4 shows how discussions within tv fandom might lead to the establishment of cooperative relationships.

Extract #2

hello everyone. How do I convert a regular translation file(divx) to 720p. i have a srt file for a dvdrip movie but the movie i have is BRrip now i want to convert the subtitle from dvd rip to BRrip please help.

Give subtitle and video the same name and see if it fits. You might be lucky. If the subtitle is off sync, have a look at our tutorials about syncing subtitles. There is no difference between syncing a subtitle for a DVDrip or 720p mkv.

Unfortunately, I tried but did not fit. Why is there no difference. then why I see many people are asking to submit a copy of the subs for 720p

Well, then you have to resync it. As I said, have a look at the tutorials. You can use subtitle workshop or time adjuster for this task. Don't forget to upload the result. :-)

Extract #3

Dear Arab translators, I suggest that we make this page a forum for reporting the movies we are translating. Of course, some of us will decide not to translate a certain movie when we know that another good translator is already working on it. This will save our time and efforts and result in translating more films and allowing other subscribers to know the movies we are translating and wait for our translations. If any translator still wants to translate a movie although another translator has reported that he is working on it, there is no problem of course. Thanks for all your efforts and your valueable time.

Extract #4

Hi Mr Bibou thanks for your comments. Lost is really a great show so far. Apart from the sci-fi element, it has supreme actings that make you feel for the characters. I used to watch Stargate SG-1 and after watching 10 seasons you could tell the actors were getting tired into the show and became sloppy in acting. I mean how could you be entertained when they stepped into an unknown territory like they were walking a dog in the park?

I picked 24 [as one of my favourite series] for many reasons. It has great actings, fast-pacing stories, believable logics, near-the-future technologies, new villians for each season and everything you need to keep on watching. In fact the show could go on without Jack Bauer because a show with real-time concept could apply to many themes!

ya you where wright. and let me tell you that every have his interst and
his ideas about what he like watch and what dislike. and you are free to
watch every things you want and there is no one who can tell you why.
and i hope so if we can working toghether in the near future.

The two following extracts are illustrations of discourse relating to matters
of language, translation and interpretation. Extract #5 shows how input on
translations of a particular software developed within the community (Sub-
Downloader) from a French-speaking participant makes her or him an official
translator for that language.

Extract #5

Posted: Wed Jun 06, 2007 6:00 pm Post subject: SubDownloader trans-
lation errors
  Hi, This topic is to report translation errors in SubDownloader...
Please report the concerned language!

I have a little one here: French translation: when uploading a subtitle,
the message in the popup window says something like "en cours d'envoir,
patience....".. envoir is misspelled, it should be "envoi" (without the
"r"). I think that the first letter of the sentence is in small caps too, it
should be upper case ...

login, and you can correct it. you are now official french translator, welcome to our team

Extract #6 consists of part of a discussion thread about the Thai queer ro-
mantic drama film *The Love of Siam*. The extract shows how subscene participants from different cultural backgrounds deal with both the technical and
sociocultural aspects of the subtitling of this movie.

Extract #6

One scene from the directors cut that i wasn't quite sure of (and maybe
im being stupid) when Mew and Tong were sitting on the bench indoors
chatting and mew asks if he's different from other people, and then he
says "no, i mean my ummm errr...." What's that about?

hey. the two gay torrent websites that I am aware of (and I am sure there are many), both of them have versions of the subtitles that we made. I have even posted a torrent with the subs hard encoded on a couple of websites including mininova and the piratebay. There were a couple different versions of our subs because we wanted to make sure we got it right and then I took it upon myself to try and make the dialogue flow a bit better and kind of "americanized it" so people could better understand what was trying to be communicated . . . . . . um . . . err . . . um . . . errr . . . . .

Yeah, that scene on the bench I have NO EARTHLY CLUE what the hell they are talking about. I mean, how fricken vague and detached can you be . . . . . If you know what they are discussing, I wish you or someone else would share it with me. One thing I love, and hate at the same time, about this movie is that you are left to try and interpret what the hell is going on. Hell, for all I know, Mew was talking about his shoe size. Well, I . . um . . . err . . . . ummm. errr . . . . well, err,, ... ummm . . . (what is all that sh*t about, is that how they talk over there?) NOT that there is anything wrong with that. If you have the ability to email the subs you got from your friend, I would be greatful. I really just want to see if they are a version of the ones we generated and I could figure that out very quickly. (I just need to look at the dialogue)

Well i've listened to it a couple of times, and it seems the umm errr is correctly translated! i will ask a thai friend if they can throw any light on it. I wondered if it Mew was actually referring to his sexuality here, in this scene. And Tong confirms that it doesn't matter to him.

Ive emailed, but dont know how to attach when sending through here.

If both my sources were from here, it was interesting some of the differences, how come? One that stood out was the scene with the dolls by the christmas tree. In one version the mother says: do as you please which has a very different sentiment in english from the better version "do what you think is best for you." Mostly little differences like that.

Hey, i am from China. I saw this director cut version for a couple of times, and i have both chinese and english subtitles. I think my english subtitle should be pretty much the same as yours. From my understanding to this scene is that Mew is referring to his sexuality here, he want to know whether Tong think he is a little bit gay, but Tong didn't get it, he said Mew is no different than anyone else.

I would agree but did Tong get it or not? Tong seems to be a bit vague but I think he gets what Mew is saying. I did not actually think Mew was asking that because I did not think that Mew even thought of himself that way at that time. Thanks for resounding.

Reading through the different threads of the forum, I found two main types of discussions. First, those focused on collaboration. These threads consist of a first post from a user stating the aim of the thread; for example: "I suggest that we make this page a forum for reporting the movies we are translating. [...] This will save our time and efforts and result in translating more films and allowing other subscribers to know the movies we are translating and wait for our translations" (cf. extract #3). Extracts #7–9 are examples of this form.

Extract #7

i started doing "The Duchess" but i just checked and seems like Abu Essa had a great sub so I'm yet to translate a movie :) I will ! someday :DD

Extract #8

[...] PS : within two days The Office US s05e11 will be ready .

Extract #9

due to personal reasons, I'm not gonna be doing any more subtitling for the time being until ..well I'm not sure until when. sorry i couldn't reply any of my msgz or emails in the past two weeks .

Within this context, discussions tend to be devoted to coordination (cf. extract #7), information (cf. #8, 9), and—quite prominently—regulation (cf. #10–14) in relation to the communal flow of subtitles being produced on the scene.

Extract #10

I'm sorry CosTantEn , But I've checked about your movie and i found
out that it's a porn movie :S:S [...] also i checked on the actors & ac-
tresses in this movie and i found out that they are porn stars. plz , correct
me if I'm wrong and plz BE MORE CAREFUL

Extract #11

Dear users, as I stated 2 weeks ago, starting today MARCH 1ST we'll
begin to delete all the links to other sites, no matter what. I hope you all
fixed your uploads, because we won't be able to retrieve them. And
please avoid to complain about your disappearing posts because you had
2 weeks to fix them. Please also remember that links have been strictly
forbidden, and those who keep posting them could suddenly not be able
to login anymore without notice. Thanks.

Extract #12

I really feel so sorry for all of you guys who have to suffer because of the
dumb f**** who can't seem to understand what GIVING CREDIT and
NOT UPLOADING TO STREAMING SITES mean. [...] I really hope
that this horrible situation can be resolved and that those idiots wake up
and realize that what they are doing is WRONG!

Extract #13

For the third time: I already explained this. You're saving your text files
in a different encoding than what the program expects. Either you're saving them as utf-8/Unicode and it expects Latin-1 or viceversa. [...] I'll
refrain from answering now and unsubscribe from this thread, as it obviously has no further point (I've repeated myself three times at least).

Extract #14

It is obviously clear that many members of this community are lazy. [...]
If Rollins says not to take his works and abuse it, he would like to believe

that people would listen to him and use his works accordingly. But no [. . .] Obeying the wishes of someone is the only thing we have left in this corrupt, polluted Internet. If you people can't even do something as simple as that, then I'm afraid of what you're capable of doing elsewhere— within your family, at school or at the workplace. [. . .] I don't know who Rollins is. Never met him, never PM'd him. I don't know if he's a guy or a gal. Regardless, if Rollins says not to mistreat his works, and I use his works for enjoyment, I'm going to obey his wishes. What's so difficult about that?

The Damn Rules

All in all, however, the analysis of the written discourse of the subscene suggests that this setting is a successfully realized form of participatory culture as Jenkins et al. define it (2009, p. 4), an affinity space in the terminology of Gee (2005), and a pooling of collective intelligence (Lévy, 1999). It is a site of informal learning and collective problem-solving—a space for disrupting traditional patterns of media distribution, cultural transmission, and content interpretation. Skills for correctly and efficiently using subtitling tools are acquired, developed, and traded on this arena. Furthermore, knowledge is generated, notes are compared, and the reliability and credibility of various sources of information are constantly evaluated.

But it is also a site of negotiation where participants must be able to discern the social codes, grasping and following certain norms (Jenkins et al., 2009, p. 4). In other words, then, the culture of the subscene—if we read it as an expression of networked participation—is an example of "socialized cyberculture" (Fuchs, 2008, pp. 327–328) where communication and collaboration stands at the center. If we assume a different perspective, however, it could just as well be described in terms of "alienated cyberculture," where rules for inclusion/exclusion are rather strict and there is even a politics of "instilling fear" (Fuchs, 2008, pp. 328–330).

Extract #15

Before posting, please read the damn rules!! The first user may not be correct with the answer, so don't depend on his answer if you know it.

Extract #16

What do everyone think about machine translated subs? Personally it annoys me when people upload subs translated by a machine or online translator, the quality is just not good enough. To many errors and things that makes no sense for the person who reads it. Just today someone uploaded a hole bunch of Danish subs that was made with a machine, none of them made any sense, and some of them already existed in good quality translated by human. I rated all of them bad, if it was up to me such subs should be removed. What do you think?

Thank you for bringing this subject up. We've been "pleading" with uploaders to refrain from uploading such nonsensical translations, but unfortunately nothing doing. They keep wasting everybody's time, including theirs. Several posts were written to this effect, but nobody bothers to read. Upon recurrence, such uploaders are eventually banned from the Site. Please rate such subs "fake," because that's what they are. Thanks

Extract #17

if you have read a bit this forum, you should know, that requests are forbidden. For requests look at http://www.opensubtitles.org/request—add your requests there and not here. Topic, as 100 others—LOCKED.

It might seem an exaggeration to interpret such corrective discourse in terms of alienation, exclusion, and fear, but these examples show that there are indeed limits and regulations on the subscene: "read the damn rules"; "refrain from posting [what is defined as] nonsensical translations"; "you should know that requests are forbidden." In many respects, this scene adheres to rules similar to those of the so-called warez scene, where pirated software is ripped, cracked, and released. This is a form of gift economy that abides by its own logic. Paraphrasing Rehn (2004, p. 363):

What interests [the core of] participants is not the direct acquiring of specific [subtitles] (although this can be a consequence), but the way in which reputation and status can be obtained through being noticed as a particularly good source [. . . .] Managing to keep up a constant supply of

new [subtitles] in a timely fashion, or distributing these efficiently en-
sures a participants status, but only provisionally, as the scene is engaged
in these contests on a continuous basis.

From this perspective, virtue in the subscene lies in the efficient propagation
of objects that are symbolically important in this arena. The key participants
can be conceived of as a "powerless elite" (Tulloch, 1995) between, on one
side, "the power of the industry" that produces the tv series and films, and on
the other, their peers and "the general public," on whose recognition in the
form of downloads and support they rely. No matter how powerless they may
be from this perspective, they nonetheless constitute an elite. They possess a
form of symbolic capital (to use the Bourdieusian concept) that is needed "to
play for" the social field of the subscene—a field that, like any other, has a
"specific logic" that "determines those who are valid in this market" and "pertinent and active in the game in question" (Bourdieu, 1984, pp. 112–113).

Rival Generosity

This chapter has looked closely at the online practice of creating and distributing subtitle files for pirated movies and tv series. The analysis of the discursive exchange showed that the subscene is about networked collaboration,
but on quite regulated terms. This regulation comes from lead users—coordi-
nators, experts, moderators—within the forum; the act of sanctioning actions
constitutes a central part of the interaction. All in all, the patterns identified
may be read in terms of collective intelligence (Lévy, 1999), pooled knowledge, and coordinated peer production (Benkler, 2006), but also in terms of
a battle for recognition within an "ongoing process of rival generosity"
(Rehn, 2004, p. 365). Certainly, many of the forum threads are about efficient
coordination, but at the same time, they are about users signaling their individual excellence in a game of honor and responses to challenges (Bourdieu,
1990, pp. 100–101).

Once again, we arrive at the conclusion that the culture of the subscene si-
multaneously bears characteristics of "socialized" and "alienated cyberculture"
(Fuchs, 2008, pp. 327–330). This is neither a surprise nor a contradiction. As
Lovink (2002, p. 5) writes, one must be fully aware that the development of
digital culture "is happening within society with all its layers of social [...] relations." The dual processes of socialization and conflict—the interplay be-

tween unity and discord—must be seen as the basis for the social integration and development of any group.

As Simmel (1908, p. 75) puts it, it would be just as unrealizable if a group lacked any "repulsive [or] destructive [...] energies" as if it "were deprived of the forces of cooperation, affection, mutual aid, and harmony of interest." Social structure as such is, in fact, the result of this interplay: "Relations of conflict do not by themselves produce a social structure, but only in cooperation with unifying forces. Only both together constitute the group as a concrete, living unit" (p. 77). And, "what the observer or the participant himself thus divides into two intermingling trends may in reality be only one" (p. 79).

· 7 ·

HOLY SHIT! IT WORKS!!

I can suddenly become relieved when someone else in an online exchange is getting pounded or humiliated, because that means I'm safe for the moment. If someone else's video is being ridiculed on YouTube then mine is temporarily protected. (Lanier, 2010, p. 60)

Disruptive spaces exist. Even fluid and volatile network spatialities have the potential to function as sites of mobilization (cf. chapter 4). When assessing this potential, however, we must keep in mind that such spaces are involved with other spaces in a game of symbolic struggle and domination (cf. chapter 5). Furthermore, when we are talking about digital disruption, we must also take into account the hybrid relations in the politics of the online/offline (cf. chapter 6). As chapter 6 shows, the multidimensionality of social space (Bourdieu, 1985) means not only that spaces are ordered in relation to each other, but also that agents within spaces are engaged in a symbolic game of status and social regulation.

In this chapter we look at the empirical case of user comments on YouTube, focusing on the processes by which various types of content are

met by various types of reactions occupying differential positions in the social space of YouTube discourse. This is in keeping with this book's argument that digital culture must be addressed as practice. As Bourdieu (1984,
p. 244) writes:

> To escape from the subjectivist illusion, which reduces social space to
> the conjectural space of interactions, that is, a discontinuous succession
> of abstract situations, it has been necessary to construct social space as
> an objective space, a structure of objective relations which determines
> the possible form of interactions and of the representations the interac-
> tors can have of them.

One such objective space where social negotiations on "possible forms"
and "representations" are ongoing is YouTube. This is surely a social media
site rather than—as its early tagline stated—a mere video repository. The site
has a number of built-in social networking features (Ellison & Boyd, 2007)
by which it enables various forms of interaction, including options to comment on and rate videos, as well as to comment on and rate the comments
themselves. It also supports "likes," "friending," and subscription. YouTube
can be seen as "a social networking site, with the added feature of hosting
video content" (Paolillo, 2008). Accounting for somewhere around 20% of
all http traffic and almost 10% of all Internet traffic (Cheng, Dale, & Liu,
2008), YouTube is definitely at the center of the "social media revolution." It
is no surprise, then, that the last few years have seen an upsurge in YouTube
scholarship (Burgess & Green, 2009; Lovink & Niederer, 2008; Snickars &
Vonderau, 2009). In particular, the comments on videos are an interesting
source of data that can be mined and mapped in order to generate information about the interaction between users and the social and discursive codes
governing this social space.

Affinity, Trolling, and Hating

Posting comments on YouTube is a way of manipulating "interpretive access"
(Lange, 2008, p. 361) to the phenomena, acts, and identities on display in the
clips. The YouTube comment threads therefore constitute one of the more important social arenas online today. But the understanding of practice in this
media place is double-sided, based on coexisting notions of "socialized" versus

"alienated cyberculture" (Fuchs, 2008). While the potential of YouTube is celebrated by some, others claim that traditional and elitist conceptions of authorship, publicness, and aesthetics work as a sort of conservative power among users of the site (Müller, 2009). Jones and Schieffelin (2009, p. 1062) summarize the duality:

> While some view this internet forum as having the potential to provide a positive multimedia participatory environment, others claim that YouTube's comment forums are the most "loud" and "dumb" corner of the Internet. For those who must read the comments, but are offended by the form that they take, a Firefox extension called the YouTube Comment Snob has been created to eliminate comments that exhibit nonstandard forms. The application of this extension would eliminate most of the [. . .] comments [. . .] leaving us with little textual material to consider.

This chapter is set in the force field between images of YouTube as, on the one hand, a platform for open exchange, peer support, and creativity, and on the other, a disciplinary space of symbolic violence (Bourdieu, 1991). Clearly, the discourse of YouTube comment threads does not have the same cultural weight as many other media outlets, but it is nonetheless interesting in its own right. Jones and Schieffelin (2009, pp. 1062–1063) write:

> Much like bathroom graffiti [. . .], the potential for anonymity that YouTube affords opens the commenting forums to a wide array of voices, but participants carefully scrutinize the style of their own comments and each other's. Unlike graffiti, YouTube comments tend to retain a high degree of topical coherence, if not a cumulative progression or structure of responsive turntaking.

The point here is that although the relatively disinhibited climate in the threads allows for extreme discourse, the negotiation of social rules and the formation of coherent discursive patterns still take place. While communication in online media circuits and affinity spaces clearly has a social potential, scholars have warned that there are patterns in online communication that reflect a "broader trend towards diminished concern with how we present ourselves to others," and that there is a "growing acceptance of whatever other people say or think" (Baron, 2005, p. 21). This notion is formulated by Suler

(2004) as "the online disinhibition effect." Suler starts from the insight that people tend to say and do things online that they would not do face-to-face. While one outcome of this may be unusual generosity and kindness, or openness that brings people closer to each other, there are also negative forms of disinhibition: "We witness rude language, harsh criticisms, anger, hatred, even threats. Or people visit the dark underworld of the Internet—places of pornography, crime, and violence—territory they would never explore in the real world" (Suler, 2004, p. 321).

The disinhibition is a consequence of a number of factors. First, although system operators, geeks, and motivated users can always find out things about others, the Internet is a place of relative invisibility and anonymity, which may lead to dissociation and less responsible behaviors. Second, the asynchronicity of much online communication means that users do not have to deal with people's immediate reactions. Third, psychological processes of solipsistic introjection ("it's all in my head") and dissociative imagination ("the online is another, fictional, world") also increase disinhibition, according to Suler. In practice, the degree of disinhibition of individuals will of course vary; indeed, the factors discussed above may make some people insecure and thus cautious and hesitant in online interactions.

Applying these ideas specifically to YouTube comments, many of Lange's (2008) interviewees reported that "hating" was a major problem on the site. Haters are users who post negative, provocative comments rather than simply critical (or helpful) remarks. These comments often are completely disconnected from the content of the video, and in this respect, too, they differ from comments containing constructive criticism or sincere assistance in helping the author better his or her technique. Hating is a form of "trolling." Trolling, carried out by individuals labeled "trolls," refers to posting with the aim of disrupting online discussion spaces and luring participants info fruitless arguments (Donath, 1999; Herring, Job-Sluder, Scheckler, & Barab, 2002; Lanier, 2010). Troll postings include apparently foolish contradictions of common knowledge, deliberately offensive insults, and pointless requests (Bond, 1999). This chapter investigates YouTube comments discourse in the force field between discourses of affinity and discourses of trolling and hating. The extent to which these two discourses are employed will be measured through sentiment analysis.

I shall first try to determine the types of sentiments that characterize YouTube comments discourse, and also how positive and negative sentiments interact discursively in the comments. To do this, a dataset of 24,000 com-

Table 5: Dataset Including Comments on Videos from Six Popular Genres

Title	Genre	Views	Comments	Comments analyzed
Obama's Contentious Fox News Interview	news	128,085	5,870	4,000
Watch This! Gaming: Top 5 Plays in Modern Warfare 2: Ep 4 (Gameplay Video)	gaming	721,923	4,113	4,000
Lady Gaga - Bad Romance	entertainment	303,905,643	679,613	4,000
I'm Starbuck from BSG...dorkiest vlog ever (supanova)	blogs	794,046	12,083	4,000
Adora's goth make-up tutorial #1	how-to	960,167	5,330	4,000
Welcome to China	travel	498,573	15,005	4,000

ments was collected using the Web Info Extractor software. The selection was guided by the categorization of YouTube videos presented by Sharma and Elidrisi (2008). Among the twelve existing predefined genre classifications available at the time of their study, six were identified as the most common in an analysis of tagging practices. These genres are how-to, blogs, travel, news, entertainment, and gaming. YouTube's search function was used to identify the most commented-on videos in each genre. From these, one video from each genre was selected based on the intensity of the comments it elicited. The videos analyzed are listed in Table 5.

To get a picture of the sentiments, positive and negative, expressed in the comments, a method for sentiment strength detection in short informal text was used (Thelwall, Buckley, Paltoglou, & Cai, 2010). The SentiStrength opinion-mining algorithm is designed to extract positive and negative emotion from sentences, and was specifically developed with the grammar and spelling styles of online communication in mind.

Following the sentiment analysis, I look more closely at comments discourse relating specifically to the how-to genre; it is this type of video that elicited the most positive comments. It is important to note that the how-to genre is very broad, representing a wide variety of how-to videos related to a multitude of user groups and activities. But for the purposes of this study, I look at the phenomenon of how-to videos in general. Ten how-to videos were selected based on their popularity and with the aim of including a variety of different sorts of clips within the wider genre. As a point of comparison, similar material consisting of comments on popular news videos was also collected.

News videos were defined as videos that are released on YouTube channels of corporate media outlets, or user videos that are simply extracts or copies of such material. The first 1,000 comments posted on each of these videos were analyzed (Table 6). Focusing finally on the 10,000 comments relating to the set of ten how-to videos, CCA will be used.

Table 6: Dataset Including Comments on Ten How-to Videos and Ten News
         Videos

Title	Genre	Views	Comments	Comments analyzed
How to Pick a Lock	how-to	2,441,970	4,832	1,000
How to Moonwalk Tutorial	how-to	8,171,176	12,082	1,000
How to Fold a T-shirt in 2 Seconds	how-to	4,004,297	7,907	1,000
How to Draw a "Realistic" Manga Face	how-to	1,791,347	5,672	1,000
How to Clear Blackheads Dirty Pores on Nose	how-to	513,650	1,324	1,000
How to Solve a Rubik's Cube (Part One)	how-to	16,917,340	29,740	1,000
How to Wolf Whistle	how-to	1,693,839	3,083	1,000
How to Tie a Tie - Expert Instructions on How to Tie a Tie	how-to	5,090,297	5,898	1,000
Adora's Goth Make-up Tutorial #1	how-to	960,340	5,330	1,000
How to Catch Mew in Pokemon Red, Blue & Yellow - Walkthrough	how-to	403,924	1,777	1,000
Mysterious Missile Launches over Southern California	news	491,189	2,233	1,000
Earthquake Destruction	news	5,403,291	3,237	1,000
CNN Confirms Israel Broke Ceasefire First	news	225,576	6,141	1,000
Fox News: Palin Didn't Know Africa Was a Continent	news	1,878,086	10,193	1,000
A Closer Look at the iPhone	news	12,274,898	4,203	1,000
Sarkozy au G8	news	7,455,430	1,146	1,000
UFO Crash Hits Wind Turbine	news	5,379,537	18,382	1,000
Toxic Toys: A Poisonous Affair	news	4,919,132	1,378	1,000
BBC News - June 4, 1989, Tiananmen Square Massacre	news	786,477	4,903	1,000
Hurricane Report	news	345,864	1,245	1,000

You're Obviously Pretty . . .

We turn first to the question of what types sentiments characterize the YouTube comments discourse. Based on the analysis of 24,000 comments spread over six popular genres, the first result is that positive and negative sentiments interact throughout. Utterances and formulations that include both positive and negative evaluations, often within the same sentence, are quite common. SentiStrength gives every sentence two scores: one for positive sentiment (1 to 5) and one for negative sentiment (-1 to -5). A sentence with a score of 5/-1 is to be interpreted as strongly marked by positive sentiment; one yielding 2/-4 is primarily negative in terms of emotional content. Frequently, sentences in the analyzed dataset were ambiguous and hard to place unequivocally on either side of this continuum. The three following excerpts are examples of this:

> you're obviously pretty and your hair is pretty badass, but your eyebrows are fucked and all that extra stuff is just too much (comment to the goth make-up video; score 3/-3).

> Nat, I thought you were a loser before, but I really had no idea. I love you so much more now (comment to the blog video; score 3/-3).

> such great oratory skills. i just hope our generation can master the art. its sad because our generation our losing the passion for eloquence and speech and we need people like abraham lincoln, pres, Obama and caesar (comment to the Obama video; score 2/-4).

Looking at the full dataset, only 0.5% of the comments were maximum positive (score 5/-1)—"Awesome, girl, fucking awesome!"; "that vid is soo amazing. it's fucking awesome dude. i love it." At the other end of the spectrum, none of the comments scored (1/-5), and only 1.5% of the comments were maximum negative (1/-4)—"God will rape the lesbians and kill the gays"; "you are such a mother fuckin asshole racist." The vast majority (83%) of the comments were in the span of 1 to 3 positive and -1 to -2 negative.

There were, however, some interesting differences in the score patterns when the data were broken down by video genre. Figure 11 is a visualization of the average sentiment scores for the 4,000 comments analyzed for each of the six videos. In the far left of the figure, the video that got the most positive response in this dataset was the how-to video on applying goth make-up. It

Figure 11. Sentiment analysis of comments on videos representing different genres.

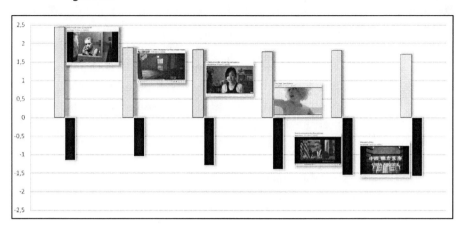

averaged just below 2.5 on the positive scale, and a little more than -1 on the negative side. Comments on the gameplay walkthrough video and the videoblog followed a similar pattern, but with slightly more moderate scores on both sides. At the other end, the music video and the news and travel clips yielded more neutral results of about 1.5/-1.5. The differences are not great by any means, especially not around the middle of the spectrum, but viewing the general pattern in the figure from left to right, it is clear that the comments on the three user-created videos (on the left) have a higher degree of positive affirmation than the comments on the three traditionally produced clips (on the right). Even though this analysis is based on a large sample of 24,000 comments, it must be remembered that the genre comparison relies on the strategic selection of these six particular clips.

To further investigate this pattern, and to try to validate the preliminary conclusion that user-created videos elicit more positive responses than other types of videos on YouTube, a sentiment analysis was performed on the 10,000 comments on ten different how-to videos. For the sake of comparison, the 10,000 comments on ten news videos were also collected. The visualization of the sentiment analysis of these videos in Figure 12 confirms the results discussed above. Most comments fall within the zone of circa 1/-1, which is indicative of the fact that comments discourse in general is not very affective. The majority of comments yield balanced sentiment scores, painting a picture of the discursive climate as generally nonpolemic (values close to 0) and nuanced (similar patterns on both sides of the 0 level).

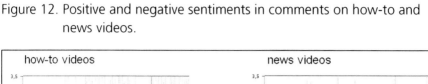

Figure 12. Positive and negative sentiments in comments on how-to and news videos.

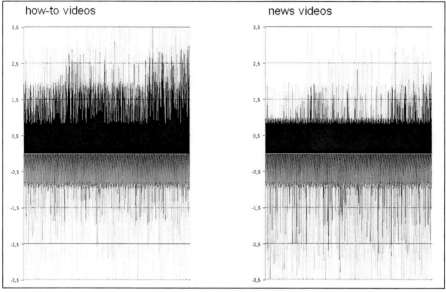

If one considers the relatively extreme zones (1.5 and up/-1.5 and below) in the figure, it is clear that the more positive sentiments have a higher intensity in the graph of how-to videos. Symmetrically, the intensity is higher on the negative side in the news videos graph.

Knowledge through Connection

In light of these indications that user-created how-to videos elicit a more positive response than much of the other content on YouTube, it is pertinent to look more closely at the inner workings of the specific space constituted by comments in this genre. Therefore, a CCA was carried out using the same 10,000 how-to video comments. The aim of this analysis was to get a picture of how various moments are relationally positioned within this discursive formation, and furthermore to uncover the underlying structures of meaning governing the individual acts of commentary.

Figure 13 is a visualization of the analyzed discursive formation. It consists of four clusters, two of which are closely connected to each other. The sizes of

Figure 13. The discursive space of YouTube comments on how-to videos.

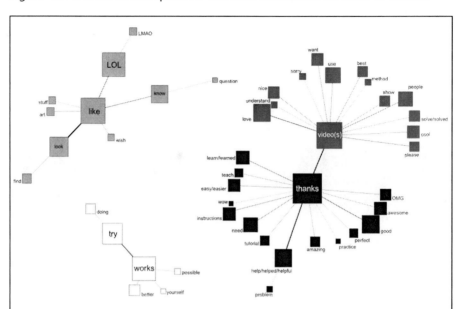

the square icons representing content themes indicate the frequency with which words, concepts, or formulations occur. The width of the connecting lines indicates the strength of the connections between themes, in terms of co-occurrences—the more frequently a conceptual pair appears together in one and the same comment, the thicker the line. Lines representing fewer than five co-occurrences have been filtered out. Furthermore, an operation to retain only the one strongest relationship upheld by any given concept was performed prior to visualizing the network.

The first prominent cluster in this discursive formation (in light gray) is centered on the verb *like* and positive exclamations typical of Internet language, such as LOL and LMAO. This cluster also includes references to finding and knowing "stuff," and to posing questions. Second, the white cluster constitutes discourse about "doing" things "yourself" and getting things to "work." Finally, the two large paired clusters (the black and the dark gray conceptual categories) are organized around the key concepts of "video(s)" and "thanks." Together, they constitute the most nodal part of the analyzed discursive space as a whole, comprising a composite of positive exclamations ("cool," "nice," "wow," "love," "perfect," etc.) and the exchange of knowledge ("please," "need," "want"; "help" ➤ "method," "show," "instructions," "tutorial," "teach" ➤ "solved," "understand," "thanks"). In the following section I qualitatively analyze this discourse of helpfulness and knowledge transfer more closely.

A look at the actual content of comments on the how-to videos suggests that in spite of the quite fluid and sometimes seemingly random character of communication on YouTube, there are indeed social forces keeping the discursive spaces of the comment threads together. This is quite striking, given the immensity of the site. Grusin (2009) writes of its infinitude in terms of "the YouTube sublime":

> Browsing YouTube produces something like the experience of what I would characterize as the YouTube sublime. The number of videos on YouTube is almost too large to comprehend. Especially in print, televisual and networked news media, this sublimity is expressed in various permutations of the following sentence: "The video of X attracted more than Y million views on YouTube." When I googled [. . .] "[m]ore than," "views" and "YouTube" [it] gave me 159,000,000 hits. The rhetorical force of such numbers is to produce something like the feeling of what Kant characterized as the "mathematical sublime." Experiencing the YouTube sublime, the mind is unable to conceive the immensity of the YouTube universe even while it is empowered by the experience of an affective awe in the face of such immensity. (Grusin, 2009, pp. 60–61)

Observing this immensity, one wonders about the nature of the social space constituted through the discourse of the comments. Can one speak of the communicative contexts surrounding the how-to videos in terms of any form of community, commitment, or engagement? Although there is no evidence in the data for the existence of community in terms of close-knit personal ties among participants, there are certainly indications that this is a virtual space adhering to specific social rules and customs. It can be conceived of as an affinity space (Gee, 2005). By focusing on the dimensions of space and place instead of on community, attention is directed away from the idea of a coherent and reasonably stable group of participants. Rather than getting stuck in questions about boundaries—about who is in, and who is out—the notion of affinity spaces allows us to focus on the studied context as a space for structured activity, no matter the number or the heterogeneity of the actors.

oh my god this thing is so helpful i can do it now thanks thanks

thanks for the help! the demonstrations were very helpful!

it took me about half an hour but i did it! i dont like the way people bitched about you're amazing intelligence. if they didn't like it, they didnt need to continue watching.

can you make more vids plz? n you hav a really pretty smile by the way by the way

Nice vid. i think im gonna try it out now now. Thanks for posting it.

Comments such as these demonstrate that the how-to videos are met with thanks and encouragement fed back to the author of the video. In addition to this, it is also common for commentators to support the authors when they get malevolent responses from some users. It seems that the affinity spaces constituted through comments discourse on how-to videos on YouTube are based largely on the socialized (as opposed to alienating) forms of cyberculture (Fuchs, 2008, pp. 227–234). The comments quoted above are examples of how gratitude for the instructive demonstrations is strongly expressed; many users also say that they are going to try doing these things themselves after watching the videos.

I have always wanted to learn how to do this, and I'm looking forward to trying this out! No, not for anything illegal! I have 3 children and money is tight. I don't have money for a locksmith if myself, my husband or even one of our children lose the keys. =) Thanks for the lesson! [comment to the lockpicking tutorial].

This is sweet cuz my step mom hates how I fold my T-shirts. I shall learn this new skill and use it to slay dragons. or not [comment to the t-shirt folding tutorial].

In addition to the many positive responses, users sometimes provide the authors of the videos with balanced, polite, and constructive criticism.

No offence to uploader, but this is a very bad guide for begginers. to explain to begginers, you must explain the logic behind every move. not simply ask them to learn algorithms. i learnt how to solve the rubicks cube, and im proud to say that i did so without the use of any algorithms. once you understand the logic behind what your doing, you can find shortcuts and make up your own unique algorithms. the understanding is the key rather than blindly memorizing someone else's understanding of it [comment to the Rubik's cube tutorial].

Furthermore, many users come back to the thread to report on their attempts to follow the tutorials. From the perspective of fragmented cyberculture, one might have expected that people wanting to master a specific skill would simply search out the video, use it, and move on with their lives. On the contrary, not only do many take the time to post a "thanks" to the author, but a substantial group of commentators also return to the thread for a debriefing.

Holy Shit! It Works!!

thanks a bunch! i learned how to moonwalk from this vid. some of my friends say its kinda cheesy learning off of utube but hey its a way! laugh out loud this video is perfect if you want to know how to do the moonwalk [comment to the moonwalking tutorial].

Lol, i unlocked my brothers room today using a bobby pin. hahaha [comment to the lockpicking tutorial].

this helped the most out of all the things i've seen in the last year. Your an amazing drawer [comment to the manga drawing tutorial].

Wow! Amazing, i tried it and now i cant see a single blackhead on my nose ! Thanks Thanks [comment to the blackhead removal tutorial].

The above extracts exemplify how people who make use of the videos return to the comment threads to communicate their experiences back into the affinity space. Many of these acts of feedback communication lead to more long-lived dialogues or group discussions; this confirms the view of Burgess and Green (2009, p. 63) that, although YouTube's architecture was not built to support collective participation or collaboration, a lot of "community-oriented activities" are taking place on the site. As the following comments illustrate, the how-to videos lead to group activity and interaction.

Do more eyes and lips too. Love your videos, make the whole body
please! [comment to manga drawing video]

Holy shit who sings this song? someone send me a message telling me
please!

please watch my moonwalk /watch?v=R_iFu5PdHgI

check out the rubiks cube pattern video on my channel please!

dang, it works, and if you accidently kill him, you can redo the glitch
from the start where you get seen by the trainer and then teleport away
[comment to gaming walkthrough video].

The first quote above is an example of how users ask authors for further help
on related topics, and in the second quote the background music used in a
video prompts a commenter to ask a question in the same space. The third
and fourth quotes are examples of people uploading new videos after viewing
tutorials, and the final quote shows how a user viewed a video, developed additional strategies, and returned to share them.

Microcontent and Community Building

Through a combination of sentiment analysis and CCA, YouTube user comments were analyzed to investigate which sentiments characterize this discursive space, and which genres of videos more commonly elicit positive
sentiment. The analysis of 24,000 comments on six strategically selected
videos representing different popular genres on YouTube showed small differences among the reactions to the clips. But the differences that did exist were
quite striking, as the user-created videos were more positively received than
any of the other video types.

In light of previous writings on the potential for peer support and mutual
encouragement through this type of "microcontent" (Alexander & Levine,
2008), this preliminary overview indicated that further analyses of this pattern were warranted. In the second analytical step—a CCA of a dataset of
20,000 comments distributed evenly over ten how-to videos and ten news
corporation clips—it was found once again that the user-created videos got a

more positive response than the news videos. In the final step, which focused on mapping the discursive formation constituted by the 10,000 comments on the how-to videos, four thematic clusters emerged. The first one was about posing questions and "finding" and "knowing" things, the second was about do-it-yourself culture, and the third and fourth were about help and the exchange of knowledge.

This shows that through the microcontent of YouTube comments, media circuits (Lange, 2008; Rouse, 1991) can be established. This might occur through viewers establishing more or less long-standing contacts with each other based on common interests, through viewers giving constructive criticism to authors, or through viewers refining techniques presented in a video and then posting their own videos. The media circuit created through the analyzed discourse is marked by politeness, helpfulness, and constructivity. Selective closer analyses that were made in order to validate the result confirmed this conclusion. While the vastness and fluidity of "the YouTube sublime" (Grusin, 2009) make it problematic to speak of these patterns in terms of community-building, they can be seen as evidence of the existence of affinity spaces (Gee, 2005). The YouTube comment threads offer a space for interaction where certain forms of linguistic capital (Bourdieu, 1977a) are valid, no matter who participates, or where they participate, at any given moment.

In spite of online disinhibition, trolling, hating, and other forms of content that may disrupt the media circuit, for the most part the comments discourse is quite neutral. According to the SentiStrength algorithm, 83% of the comments analyzed were between 1 to 3 positive and -1 to -2 negative. Only 1.5% of the comments were maximum negative, and closer qualitative reviews of the material confirm that this is the level at which one finds the purely malevolent comments. (It should be noted, though, that the quite straightforward sentiment algorithm is not optimal for spotting more subtle forms of negativity based on in-jokes, etc.)

Looking at the results of the analyses, Gee's theory of affinity spaces (2005) appears to be a suitable tool for understanding what is going on in the how-to comment threads. Affinity spaces are interactive sites—online or offline— where people come together through common goals, interests, or activities. Affinity spaces often emerge within various forms of fan cultures, as websites, forums, and other platforms featuring information and resources linked to a specific area of interest become interlinked through social patterns of consumption and creation. The analyzed comment threads on how-to videos exemplify the notion of affinity spaces in several ways. The common endeavor (e.g., folding a T-shirt, picking a lock, removing blackheads) is at the center, not the homogeneity of the group or the identity of participating individuals.

In sum, the comments discourse on how-to videos generates an affinity space that is characterized by interactivity, thankfulness, encouragement, and support. Of course, this is an analysis of a selection of comments on a video genre that tends to generate more dialogue in a more helpful climate than other genres. The important questions about how the power of processes such as these are or may be harnessed to effect a more substantial transformation of the public still remain. Nonetheless, this case study helps sketch an image of the participatory possibilities of YouTube media circuits. Figure 14 represents a set of ideal types of user strategies ranked by degree and type of affinity. Depending on the context, and depending on which strategies users employ and which strategies are discursively possible, YouTube comments can express anything from total passivity and detachment to deep engagement.

This chapter looked at the empirical case of YouTube comment postings, and showed that comments on user-created how-to videos are more supportive and affirming than comments on videos in several other examined genres. Further comparisons and readings of the material confirmed this result and gave a more detailed picture of how this encouraging and participatory discourse functions. While commonplace and recreational activities such as applying make-up, learning to wolf whistle, and solving the cube are not world-altering, all of these discursive processes taken together illustrate that increasingly larger groups of people are taking part in cultures of knowledge far removed from formal educational settings.

Jenkins et al. (2009) argue that the emerging affinity spaces and the participatory cultures inhabiting them are important environments for acquiring

Figure 14. Ideal types for user strategies, ranked by degree of affinity.

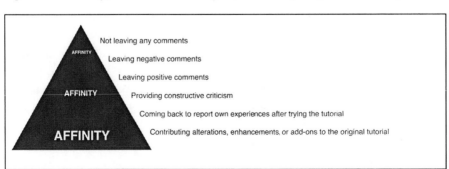

media literacies that will be essential in the future. They also claim that whereas traditional, formal education and one-to-many communications are often conservative, the collective problem-solving and peer-to-peer learning processes within the pop culture domain of sites such as YouTube are more experimental, innovative, and stimulating. Furthermore, the participant in a networked public can stay on the move, opting in and out of communities and spaces should they fail to meet their needs. Evidence for this can be found in the analyses presented in this chapter, but further critical research that looks more closely at the limits of participation is still needed. Who can participate, and who is shut out? And more concretely, how can these types of everyday participation be translated into more "serious" forms?

· 8 ·

PLURAL REACTIONS

[W]hen social differentiation and audience segmentation are the order of the day, we need take account of a plurality of reactions, each with their different constituencies, effectivities and modes of discourse. (McRobbie & Thornton, 1995, p. 564)

This chapter analyzes and discusses reactions to YouTube video clips relating to school shootings. It illustrates how, and under what conditions, comment threads on online videos can function as noise that disrupts the discourse produced by "mainstream" or "official" outlets. The chapter argues that although a moral panic reaction sequence can be clearly identified in news reporting as well as search traffic relating to issues at the intersection of digital media and school shootings, broadly applying the panic perspective produces an oversimplified picture of the emerging new media landscape where audiences play an increasingly active role as co-producers of content.

Before the school shooting at Virginia Tech in 2007 and the similar tragedies in Finland's Jokela in 2007 and Kauhajoki in 2008, the gunmen gave warnings via videos they posted on YouTube. This fact was strongly emphasized in the news media coverage of these events. TimesOnline referred, in the case of Kauhajoki, to "the YouTube Gunman," and a dangerous assumption of causality (YouTube equals massacre) was evident in the discourse. Whenever a new medium enters the arena, strikingly similar debates on basic social and cultural norms emerge, and the new medium becomes a rhetorical device in discussions that are actually about something completely different. These "media panics" (Drotner, 1999) tell us less about the discussed media than about much broader social and cultural dilemmas. The moralizing discourse about YouTube, for example, directs attention away from the fact that, for example, the United States (where Virginia Tech is located) has the highest level of gun ownership in the world, and Finland (where Jokela and Kauhajoki are located) comes in third on the same list. Gun statistics are of course only part of the equation, but all in all, the media panic mode of representation obscures the multitude of social and cultural factors that clearly contribute to the events (e.g., bullying, masculinity ideals, class differences, etc.).

This chapter looks beyond the assumption that because alarmist headlines and patterns of reporting exist, there has been (or is) an all-encompassing panic about extreme youth violence (such as school shootings) and new media (i.e., YouTube). First, I review some search engine and online news statistics in order to determine the existence and extent of a panic reaction. Second, I analyze YouTube user comment discourse on school shooting clips. The main question is whether a panic reaction sequence (Cohen, 1972, pp. 22–23) can be identified in the YouTube comment discourse.

YouTube Shootings: A Media Panic?

The ways in which the media and the public have typically responded to incidents of school shootings constitute a textbook example of the reaction sequence of the moral panic (Cohen, 1972; Goode & Ben-Yehuda, 1994). Of course this is not surprising considering the disturbing and tragic nature of these events. For obvious reasons, they generate fear and also calls for measures to be taken to prevent other tragedies. In the wake of the Columbine High School shooting in 1999, U.S. schools hired security officers and youth counselors and installed metal detectors, and Burger King discontinued a toy action figure that might have reminded people of the name of one of the school shooters. Schools arranged bullet drills, some teachers carried concealed weapons, and certain types of media content ("dangerous" music, movies, and games) were debated and controlled.

The public discussion about school shooting footage on the Internet not only gives the "moral crusaders" (Cohen, 1972, p. 127) an opportunity to stake their claims—"Experts and pundits will make claims about the purported roles of all aspects of the school shooters' life, from violent movies, video games, gun control, heavy metal music to parenting techniques and antidepressant medications" (Weisbrot, 2008, p. 147)—but also fits perfectly with the media logic. According to theories about so-called news values, the media prefers to report on crimes that are violent—"If it bleeds, it leads" (Maguire, Weatherby, & Mathers, 2002)—as well as unusual, dramatic, and sensational. School shootings, of course, fit all of these criteria, and they also fulfill the ideals of periodicity and consonance (Cohen & Young, 1973). The dramaturgical features of a school shooting story allow it to retain the public's interest over a number of days or even weeks (periodicity), and it is always possible to link the current shooting back to previous cases (consonance). Furthermore, when these events are mediated by a new technology such as YouTube, media interest is even more intensified.

Using the criteria introduced by Goode and Ben-Yehuda (1994), Burns and Crawford (1999) demonstrate that the media, the public, and politicians in consensus displayed a degree of concern and hostility that was disproportionate to the actual facts about school shootings. They claim that despite the shootings, schools remained "extremely safe places," and that violence in schools was less frequent in the late 1990s than it had been in earlier decades. The problem, according to these authors, is that the underlying social issues that lead to school shootings were not broadly assessed in their actual context. Instead, reactions focused on "isolated incidents" and became too "emotion-ally-charged" (Burns & Crawford, 1999, p. 147).

One of the basic characteristics of a moral panic reaction is that it "sud-denly appears," and then just as quickly "disappears, submerges or deteriorates" (Cohen, 1972, p. 9). Goode and Ben-Yehuda (2006, pp. 55–56) make the point that although some moral panics become routinized or institutionalized, most of them are marked by a sudden eruption, and they subside almost as quickly. Using data gathered using Google Trends, Figure 15 illustrates changes in the number of searches for "virginia tech," "jokela," and "kauha-joki." These shootings did not take place on the same day, of course, but the

Figure 15. Google searches for "virginia tech," "jokela," and "kauhajoki"
three days before and twelve days after the shootings.

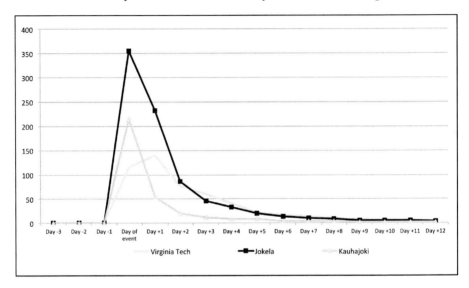

figure has been generated using an overlay technique whereby the points of
impact have been aligned. This makes it possible to evaluate the explosiveness, or eruptive power, of these reactions.

The scale on the y-axis indicates how many times these terms were searched
for in relation to how often they are searched for normally. This is because the
Google Trends data is scaled on the basis of the average search traffic of the
entered terms. This explains why the peak for Jokela is the highest and the
one for Virginia Tech is the lowest. What is interesting here, however, is not
the height of the peaks but the similarity of the reaction sequences. The general pattern is that when the shooting first occurs, Google searches skyrocket,
but after about five to six days, search traffic returns to its previous levels. This
pattern is self-evident and not surprising in any respect. Dramatic public
events generate concern as well as an interest in knowing more about what
happened, and it is also natural that interest falls abruptly after the initial need
to know has been satisfied. This pattern is by no means an indicator of a moral
panic reaction.

The main point of moral panic theory is that conditions, behaviors, per-
sons, or groups—which already existed before the reaction exploded, and
which continue to exist after the "crisis" has submerged—emerge "to become

defined as a threat to societal values and interests" (Cohen, 1972, p. 9). In other words, the interesting thing is not the peak illustrated in Figure 15, but what this peak pulls along with it. When defining the concept of "symbolization," Stanley Cohen (1972, p. 40) writes that in moral panic reactions "[n]eutral words such as place-names can be made to symbolize complex ideas and emotions; for example, Pearl Harbor [and] Hiroshima." Similarly, Weisbrot (2008, p. 847) contends that "[m]erely invoking the names of these schools is enough to introduce the topic to be discussed." What these topics are in the case of school shootings is already well-established: bullying, gun control, popular culture, mental illness, etc.

Although Burns and Crawford (1999) argue quite convincingly that reactions to school shootings follow the moral panic pattern, I have made a couple of analyses that emphasize this further, with special reference to the Internet and to more recent incidents. Figure 16 illustrates Google search traffic on two key concepts in the "panic package" relating to school shootings: gun control and Marilyn Manson (one of the musical artists most often blamed for causing the shootings). Aggregated data from the days surrounding the Virginia Tech, Jokela, and Kauhajoki shootings have been set in relation to a common timeline to show search activity from three days before to nine days after the incidents.

Figure 16. Google searches for "gun control" and "marilyn manson" three days before and nine days after the Virginia Tech, Jokela, and Kauhajoki shootings.

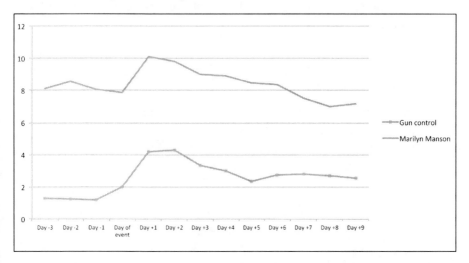

Although the values on the y-axis are much lower than in Figure 15, the similar shape of the two curves in Figure 16 is conspicuous: Search activity relating to gun control and Marilyn Manson increases immediately after the school shootings take place, and declines within around five or six days. These observations indicate that the reactions in the form of Google traffic follow a moral panic pattern. While Figure 15 illustrates the explosiveness and characteristic decline of the reaction, Figure 16 gives two (of many possible) examples of how these dramatic reactions tend to activate an entire "referential context, with all its associated meanings and connotations" (Hall, Critcher, Jefferson, Clarke, & Roberts, 1978, p. 19). This is a sign that a process of "sensitization" (Cohen, 1972, pp. 77–85) is in play. The ways in which interest in gun control and Marilyn Manson increases are examples of how the overall reaction brings issues that might otherwise have remained dormant into the social consciousness.

In other words, when one talks more of school shootings, one talks more of gun control and Marilyn Manson. School shootings are thereby articulated as a problem that has to do with a set of other things—in this example, gun control and "dangerous" music. Figure 17 illustrates an attempt to validate these observations further. It shows Google Trends data for search traffic on "media violence," "gun control," and "bullying" in 2007. At the time of the Virginia Tech shooting (April 16) there was a notable increase in interest in the gun control issue, and in the aftermath of the Jokela shooting (November 7), searches for all three themes increased. It is worth noting that we do not know for sure what caused the growing interest in these themes at these particular moments in time, but it seems very likely that there is a connection with the school shootings.

Figure 17. Google searches for "media violence," "gun control," and "bullying" during 2007.

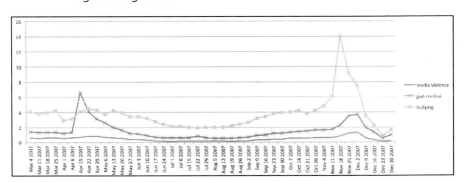

Looking closely at how search traffic relating to YouTube varies in relation to interest in the school shooting incidents, it is hard to find any obvious patterns. This is because the search volume for YouTube—one of the most visited and Googled sites on the Internet—is extremely high. After adding data on news reference volume available from Google Trends, however, a very interesting result appears. The news reference volume data is based on the number of times a particular topic appears in the Google News aggregator, which is an automated service that collects news stories from a large number of online news sources. Figure 18 shows that the news reference spike relating to Kauhajoki at the time of the shooting (September 2008) brought the level of news reference to YouTube with it. This pattern is most obvious in the case of Kauhajoki, but the graphs rendered by Google Trends when "kauhajoki" is replaced with "virginia tech" or "jokela" are quite similar.

From the perspective of discourse theory, one can interpret the spikes-within-spikes pattern as part of a process of *articulation*. There are, as we have seen, several ways of trying to understand the school shootings (as having to do with media violence, popular culture, gun control, bullying, etc.). Another way is to articulate them as incidents that have to do with YouTube—as "YouTube shootings" by "YouTube gunmen." In this case, we are dealing with the specific form of moral panic that Drotner (1999) labeled "media panic." These are panics that represent reactions to the introduction of new media. Drotner states that "[t]he computer in general and games and the Internet in particular serve as mental metaphors for discussing and debating wider social concerns" (1999, p. 594). Digital technology—the most recently introduced major media technology—clearly gives rise to strong feelings, both positive and negative. On the one hand, computers and the Internet are perceived as rational tools providing great possibilities for information searching, education, data processing, etc.; on the other hand, violent computer games, images

Figure 18. News reference volumes for "youtube" and "kauhajoki" around the time of the Kauhajoki shooting.

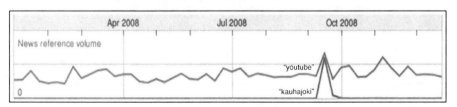

of sex and violence on the Internet, and other emotionally charged features of this technology often produce negative reactions. According to Drotner, this discursive dichotomy has re-emerged whenever new media have been introduced. This is because this dualism is "lodged within fundamental dilemmas of modernity" (1999, p. 596).

Disrupting the Panic

Let us now shift our attention to how school shooting videos are discussed and received in comments posted on the YouTube site. CCA was done on the content of the comment threads of the most commented-on clips relating to each of the four shooting incidents mentioned above. All comments entered up to September 7, 2009 (totaling 20,513) were analyzed. The clips are listed in Table 7. The comments were very unevenly distributed between the four incidents: More than half relate to the Columbine footage, while a mere 1% relates to the most frequently discussed Kauhajoki clip. This would be a huge problem if one were to apply strict criteria of representativity.

The aim of this analysis is to map the discursive space of user comments to school shooting–related footage, not to compare the number of comments on each of the incidents. Furthermore, a close review of the material

Table 7: YouTube Clips—Number of Views and Comments Registered September 7, 2009

Clip title	Type	Length	Posted	Views	Comments
Columbine Shooting Cafeteria Footage Harris Klebold					
	Security camera footage set to recordings of 911 calls.	01:39	24.11.06	2,242,130	11,308
Final Words of Virginia Tech Massacre Killer Cho Seung-Hui					
	Amateur video montage showing a photo of the shooter with his manifesto scrolling as text at the bottom of the screen while soft music is playing.	03:54	19.04.07	830,317	6,774
Jokela High School Massacre - 11/7/2007 My Message of Peace					
	Amateur video montage showing screenshots of the shooter's MySpace page and displaying (as scrolling text) a "message of peace" sent by the author of this video to the deceased shooter.	04:49	07.11.07	564,987	2,229
Matti Juhani Saari (unique video)					
	Amateur video montage including reports from ABC News, information about Finnish gun policy and statistics, and facts about the shooting.	03:13	24.09.08	62,149	202

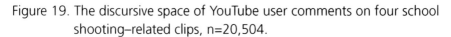

Figure 19. The discursive space of YouTube user comments on four school
      shooting–related clips, n=20,504.

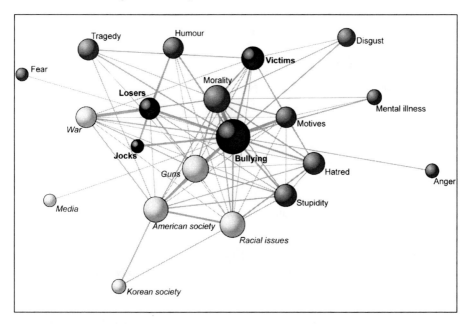

reveals that the discussion threads do not remain strictly on topic to the
original incidents. This is illustrated by the fact that Columbine happened
in 1999, six years before the launch of YouTube, and the Columbine clip included in the analysis was posted in 2006. This means that the comments
on the Columbine incident were temporally detached from the shooting itself. It is also apparent that the large comment thread on the Columbine security camera footage has served as a discussion forum about similar events
over the years. It continues to grow at an average rate of ten new posts per
day, and each of the three later shootings (Virginia Tech, Jokela, and
Kauhajoki) have been discussed in this thread. Figure 19 shows the results
of the CCA.

The figure illustrates that this discursive formation consists of three thematic subsets. First, and most nodally, the theme of bullying and the distinction between "jocks" and "losers"—prominent in Americanized high school
mythology, fictionalized and otherwise—is at the center of the discussion
(marked by dark gray vertices and bold type labels). Indeed, bullying appears
to be the nodal point around which all other discourse centers.

Eric was a fricking psychopath, i.e. no reason other than he thought that
he was superior to the rest of the human race. They were not outcasts,
they were not bullied. Everything in life does not come down to football,
hate to break it to you.

That klebold kid had a girlfriend, went to prom, and was popular. The
other kid was on the baseball team the year before. they were gun enthusiast, notice how they didn't kill any jocks or even shoot any for that
matter. Most of the kids who died were in the library.

He [Auvinen] wasn't rejected. He had friends who noticed a couple of years
ago that he started to become more and more distant. But he still had
friends before the shooting tragedy... And for the shooter, the shooting in
Jokela high school was a political statement. Sick, but he wasn't rejected.

This is a very terrible thing, and I believe no one deserves to be shot,
not preps, not bullies, not jocks, no one!! Life is High School, you just
have to deal with it

The above excerpts are illustrative of the large portions of the discussion that
are devoted to the issue of whether or not the shooters had been bullied, and
whether or not "jocks" (popular members of the athletic school subculture) had
been their targets. The first three quotes are all examples of how the outcast or
bully victim status of the gunmen is questioned and other motives are suggested
(e.g., psychopathology, gun fixation, politics). The author of the fourth quote
accepts the jocks-versus-bullies theory, but still condemns the shootings. In
these cases, then, the YouTube comment area provides users with a forum where
high school culture, bullying, and antagonisms between various groups of young
people are discussed. The discussion is often rather general, and participants
often seem to sympathize with or feel that they belong to one of these groups.

The second thematic subset (marked by medium gray vertices and labels in
roman type) consists of discourse about the trauma of the school shooting
events. This discourse focuses partly on emotional reactions (hatred, anger,
disgust, humor, tragedy, fear), and partly on trying to understand these things
in more rational terms (motives, mental illness, morality). The bullying theme
would have belonged to this latter category had it not been prominent enough
to be discussed in its own right.

this makes me feel ill to think someone could put a bullet into their classmates.

My one hope is that at least a few of you who decided to post on this video would take the time to learn more about what actually happened. To read such rants by so many ignorant people makes me feel so much sorrow for those who were actually involved in this tragedy. They deserve so much better than most of the trash I'm reading here.

RIP? u fags he [Cho] killed 32 people and made no attempt to socialize himself dont pity him your he did something wrong! god damn you people for feeling sorry for someone like this! hes a freekin physco he chose to do this he is an asshole he does not deserve the sorrow your giving him just because you saw what he said on this vid and put a sad song on it thats the only reason your saying RIP i say go to hell you son of a bitch!!!

Comments relating to this discursive theme, such as the three excerpts above, demonstrate that the YouTube comment threads on these school shooting videos allow users to express their reactions and deal with them in dialogue with others.

The third and final prominent discursive subset illustrated in Figure 19 (marked by light gray vertices and labels in italics) relates to the comments about the social and political aspects of the shootings. Guns and gun policy are discussed, as is the role of the media, and American society. Finnish society was also discussed, but far less frequently, which meant that the vertex representing that theme disappeared in a reduction of the network during earlier stages of the analysis. American society was discussed in 2,516 comments, compared to 165 comments on Finnish society. The Virginia Tech shooting also prompted some discussion of Korean society because the shooter, Seung-Hui Cho, was born in South Korea. Discourse on American society is sometimes drawn to issues of war. In these cases, U.S. culture is criticized for alleged double standards of morality:

War is just like a school shooting, only in the school..no one ever praises the shooter, but in a war they get a fuckin medal..Fuck your ideology..its filled with holes.

> LOL you pussy ass americans kill innocent soldiers DAILY in Iraq (half are your own damn people) but feel sympathetic when 13 people get shot at school. It's no wonder why the rest of the world hates you.

> And this doesn't happen in Europe? what about Finland? And in holland kids stab teachers/students on schools, so don't act like Europe is perfect with these things. The world fails with these things, not a certain part of the world.

> There was a similar shooting in Finland today, where the fuck is this world heading to? We need to fix our society otherwise we are all fucked up.

Racial issues—that is, discussions of racism, "blacks" versus "whites" versus "Asians," etc.—are also at the forefront of this discursive subset. As in many other Internet forums, racist denunciations and hard language sometimes take precedence over attempts at any deeper understanding of social relations (Coffey & Woolworth, 2004). Many of these comments are extremely offensive, and they are unified by their striving to frame the shootings in terms of race wars.

> White people didn't start shooting up schools until they went to school with niggers.

> just another whitey doing school terror—like we need any more!

> Cho Seung-Hui kiled white racists dead.

> fuck this gook mother fucker ..

Posts of this type strengthen Coffey and Woolworth's (2004, p. 12) argument that online forums are sometimes limited as a vehicle for constructive dialogue to promote understanding and address social concerns. This is especially true with dramatic and sensitive topics such as school shootings. It is also worth noting that when I did the first analyses of the material, I was struck by how many of the comments used profanity and strong language. But in spite of all this, it seems that the general function of the analyzed comment threads has been, and continues to be, to provide a platform to voice opinions about or in various other ways to deal with these tough issues. They are, in that sense, disruptive spaces providing a therapeutic and analytical alternative to the stereotyped panic reaction. Indeed, a lot of curse words are used, and the fact that extremist, classist, and racist formulations are relatively common does to some extent validate previous research on flaming (Crystal, 2001), Internet regression (Holland, 1996), and the online disinhibition effect (Suler, 2004). Still, the wide variety of themes—cf. Figure 19—cannot be ignored.

In sum, the YouTube comment threads include discussions of general problems relating to bullying and status groups in high schools, the airing of emotional reactions, and expressions of communal coping strategies. A quite striking pattern is illustrated in Figure 20, which maps how the 11,308 comments on the Columbine clip are distributed over time. The overall pattern is relatively consistent, and the number of monthly comments varies from around 300 to around 400, with peaks of activity around the times of the other school shootings. The data is somewhat inexact, because extracting these numbers from the YouTube site requires a certain amount of manual work, but clearly they suggest that comment activity on these clips is relatively constant when compared to the dramatically exploding/decaying pattern that characterizes the search traffic and news volume data previously discussed. There are some spikes, but activity never approaches zero; interest never fades in the same way public interest in the object of a moral panic declines.

Although the moral panic reaction sequence can be clearly identified in news reporting as well as search traffic relating to issues at the intersection of digital media and school shootings, the main conclusion of this chapter is that a broad application of the panic perspective oversimplifies the emerging new

Figure 20. Frequency of comments to the Columbine High School cafeteria security camera footage, with the dates of three other notable shootings marked in gray.

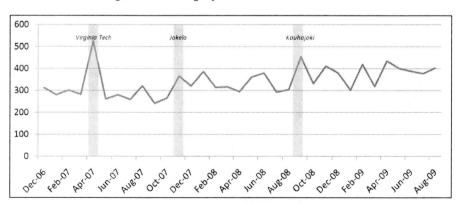

media landscape, where audiences play an increasingly active role as co-producers of content. In line with this, Angela McRobbie and Sarah Thornton (1995) suggest that the emergence of "multi-mediated social worlds" requires a revision of how moral panics are considered. Whereas Cohen's original model was developed for a society where media were univocal, and hegemonical relations were monolithic, the digital is characterized by fragmentation and multiplicity. McRobbie and Thornton argue that classic moral panic studies (Hall et al., 1978; Pearson, 1983) have a tendency to overstate the power of hegemony and social control, while understating the role played by counter-discourses.

In the age of participatory media it becomes increasingly important to "take account of a plurality of reactions, each with their different constituencies, effectivities and modes of discourse" (McRobbie & Thornton, 1995, p. 564). With this argument, McRobbie and Thornton call for an exploration of various mass, niche, and micro-media. In this chapter, I analyzed one mode of discourse in one particular medium, namely YouTube user comments on school shooting videos. The results show that the media is to a diminishing degree something that is separable from society. The analyzed texts are neither reports on, nor narratives about the school shootings in the traditional media sense. Instead, they illustrate the process wherein social reality is "experienced through language, communication and imagery" (McRobbie & Thornton, 1995, p. 570). The reality of school shootings is continuously being defined in these comment threads, as users discuss issues of bullying, high school culture, gun control, and racism, while at the same time publically, socially, and emotionally trying to deal with the trauma of these events. The comment thread thereby becomes a disruptive space, based on forms of meaning-making that oppose mainstream and ideological understandings.

· 9 ·

THE SUBACTIVIST CHALLENGE

Subactivism may or may not leak out of the small social world and be-come publicly visible, meaning that its acts and products, although mul-tiple, can remain insulated in the private sphere. This, however, does not condemn subactivism to inconsequentiality. (Bakardjieva, 2009, p. 96)

How can everyday participation be translated into a politics with the power to make a mark on society as a whole? This chapter uses the example of digital piracy to explore the question of how everyday acts of disruption or disobedi-ence in digital culture may be developed into something like a social move-ment. A starting point for this is Beck's (1997) notion of "subpolitics," which refers to the type of politics that is expressed outside of the established and tra-ditional system—and often in relation to specific issues rather than as a com-plete ideological package. Beck's point is that instead of suggesting that politics and morality are on the wane in the postmodern world, one might just as well argue that such claims are the result of a misconception of current social reality. The fact that many people have a declining interest in traditional formal poli-tics should not necessarily be interpreted as a sign that there is an actual lack of political orientation or action in society at large (cf. Mouffe, 2000). This point is illustrated by, for example, the occurrence of activities such as culture jamming and adbusting (Klein, 2000; Wettergren, 2005), online campaign organizations (e.g., avaaz.org), and hacktivism (McCaughey & Ayers, 2003).

The concept of subpolitics refers to the ways in which individual, small-scale decisions achieve political significance either because they have a direct political frame of reference, or simply because of their aggregation. The Internet has a particularly strong potential for channeling the actions of many individual users into something larger, but movements on the Internet are by nature more abstract than traditional social movements—at least at first glance—because they appear as relatively fragmented systems of joint action. In the case of digital piracy, someone in, let us say, rural Sweden downloads a file uploaded by an Internet user in Sydney; that same file is then shared with an individual in Amsterdam. There is no obvious chief ideologist or leader in this exchange, these three people have never met, and they all have their individual motivations for downloading the file (one of them simply might not care about rights issues, the second may be active in writing essays on the obsolescence of copyright, the third might just be desperately looking for a specific song or movie). With torrent technology—where only fragments of files are shared, to be reassembled by software—it gets even more complex. The consequence of this (practical) collective action is nonetheless potentially political.

Bakardjieva (2009, p. 96) develops the idea of subpolitics further, writing that "as much as Beck emphasizes forms and manifestations of politics located underneath the surface of formal institutions, his construct retains a strong public and activist element." She introduces the idea of "subactivism" as a third level of citizen participation, the first being a level of formal institutional politics and the second represented by Beck's concept of subpolitics. Subactivism, more so than subpolitics, is located in the "private sphere or the small social world" (Bakardjieva, 2009, p. 96). It relates more to personal empowerment than to political power in a strict sense. Personal empowerment is here seen as "the power of the subject to be the person that they want to be in accordance with his or her reflexively chosen moral and political standards" (p. 96). Subactivism arises spontaneously, for example in the form of new dimensions of work, homemaking, parenting, or entertainment. Bakardjieva argues that there is an ever-present potential for subactivism that can be mobilized and transformed into overt public activism through trigger events.

Another key notion of what happens when disruptive spaces are channeled into movements is found in Eyerman and Jamison's (1991) discussion of "cognitive praxis." The concept refers to the process of forming unity within a movement through the generation and dissemination of certain ideas and knowledge. According to Eyerman and Jamison, movements must be understood in terms that go beyond ideological positions or organizational programs; instead, we must focus on them as producers of knowledge and therefore producers of cultural transformations. By approaching movements as cognitive actors, we can avoid the polarization of grand theory and particularism. Once again, we must focus on practice and on how discourse is produced (cf. Bourdieu, 1990).

Cognitive praxis has three dimensions: a cosmological dimension, consisting of the movement's worldview, historical meaning, emancipatory goals, etc.; a technological dimension that consists of how the movement relates to the use of technologies; and an organizational dimension, consisting of the communicative and structural forms of movement activity. While these dimensions of cognitive practice may be implicit or unconscious to varying degrees to (sub)activists themselves, I attempt in this chapter to identify these dimensions as they emerge in the case of digital piracy, with particular emphasis on the Swedish context.

Sweden is the home country of several representatives of the pro-piracy perspective, including The Bureau of Piracy (*Piratbyrån*, hereafter TBP) and the Pirate Party (*Piratpartiet*, hereafter PP). PP is a Swedish political party founded in 2006 that inspired the creation of similar parties in several other countries. As of 2012, the party is not represented in the Swedish parliament because it did not capture enough votes in the Swedish general elections of 2006 (0.63%) or 2010 (0.65%) to meet the 4% requirement to secure a seat. However, PP received much attention both inside and outside of Sweden for winning one seat (with 7.13% of Swedish votes) in the European Parliament in 2009 (the one seat became two after the ratification of the Lisbon Treaty in December 2009). TBP was a Swedish organization founded in 2003 that worked to support people who oppose the current rules and ideas relating to copyright and intellectual property (Rydell & Sundberg, 2009). In 2003 members of TBP founded The Pirate Bay—allegedly the largest BitTorrent site of its kind in the world, and famous for the highly publicized 2009 court case against the people behind it. TBP disbanded in 2010.

The analysis in this chapter is based on research interviews from 2005 with two members of TBP, interviews from 2009 with ten young people moderately to highly engaged in digital piracy activities, and readings from TBP's website, forum, and book *Copy Me—Collected Texts from the Bureau of Piracy* (Kaarto

& Fleischer, 2005). The research material also included several TBP media appearances—in particular, two episodes of a Swedish television debate show in which representatives of TBP appeared. The first episode was from 2003, the year that TBP was founded, and the second episode was from 2005.

Digital Piracy Cultures

Online pirate culture is built upon the collective engagement of a large number of people. As Vaidhyanathan (2004, p. 21) states, the most remarkable thing is not that millions of individuals all over the world are downloading a vast number of files, but rather that large numbers of people around the globe are making an effort—cracking, sorting, copying, hosting, and distributing data. In approaching digital piracy as a social movement, one way to start is by discussing who and what should be considered part of this movement. There are many different arguments and motivations for downloading and/or uploading music, movies, and software. Should all individuals taking part in this activity be considered members of a specific social movement, and if so, do they incorporate a distinct collective identity? Drawing on interviews with young people engaged in the act of digital piracy, I have identified three ideal typical forms of digital piracy cultures: as everyday culture, political culture, and innovation culture (Lindgren, 2009).

In these interviews it became clear that for many people, digital piracy activities are associated with neither political dimensions nor legal ones. Digital piracy as everyday culture is based on a behavior taken for granted and made possible by technology that is an integral part of everyday lives. It is not necessarily associated with moral aspects. Johannes (twenty-two years old) says: "No, I don't even think about that. That it would be criminal. I've been doing file sharing for so long that I have never really thought about it that way." When I brought up the political aspects of digital piracy, I was occasionally met with skepticism. In response to the argument that under some circumstances, individual actions taken together can be described as political, Johannes replied:

> No, I wouldn't agree with that. I think it's much more about the fact that it's easy. I guess people are greedy in some ways, and if there's an easy way to get it, you try. And when the risk of getting caught is minimal . . . like . . . no, I can't agree with that.

Johan, twenty years old, although a bit more ambivalent, essentially agrees with this view (note: Simon is the interviewer/author):

> Simon: Can digital piracy be a political action to you?
>
> Johan: [pause] . . . Yes . . . maybe . . . [pause]. But most of all it's a question of access, of convenience.
>
> Simon: Some people see digital piracy as part of a political project, for example as an anti-capitalist action . . .
>
> Johan: No, that's not the case. Certainly not.

People engaged in digital piracy as unreflected everyday practice, as one way among many to consume culture, are neither directly affiliated with any social movement of any kind nor exercising self-perceived subpolitical action. Nevertheless, they are sometimes represented that way in the movement's rhetoric, as in a TBP's press release, which referred to "a powerful movement where millions of people create free access to culture."

> Simon: If, for example, a large number of individuals are sharing files, but only, like, five percent are what one could call politically aware, would you still think that the number of file sharing activities taken together could be seen as political? That for example PP could argue that:"Look! All of these people file sharing want a new society like we do!"
>
> Johan: No . . . no, I don't think so. This is, I think, putting words into somebody else's mouth . . .
>
> Simon: Yes . . .
>
> Johan: From my own perspective . . . If I were to be used like that I wouldn't think it was ok.

Johannes and Johan's views exemplify an approach where digital piracy is detached by its actors from its political aspects as well as legal and moral ones. For them, piracy is a way to consume culture and media content that in some ways is taken for granted by a generation of young people. Digital piracy as everyday culture is closely connected to Rojek's (2005) description of piracy as a new form of leisure activity. He argues that it can be interpreted as part of a new globalized leisure culture that leads to increased social inclusion and a strengthening of participation in culture and society, and that it raises important issues of justice. Seen from this perspective, one could argue that digital piracy has political aspects even if participants reject such an idea, and that this is also closely connected to Bakardjieva's notion of subactivism.

Digital piracy can be made political in many different ways. It cannot be categorized as traditionally leftist or rightist because the youth sections of all the political parties represented in the Swedish parliament in different ways have made the issue a part of their political agendas. None of the people I interviewed had clear sympathies with PP. Instead, they expressed a left-oriented rhetoric that contrasts with PP's arguments about "civic rights" and "safeguarding the privacy of the individual," and how "monopolies are harmful to society" (PP's website). One of the interviewees, Arvid (twenty-two years old), emphasized the solidarity that some of the private torrent trackers are built upon:

> Active participation in the community is rewarded, and I think that's great. It adds a whole new level to the downloading as well [...]. I don't like open trackers at all, it's like: a hundred people are exploiting ten people. Ten people that very faithfully keep their computer on, expose themselves to the risks and all that. And then a hundred people just exploiting that and giving nothing back apart from the little time that they upload, I think that's fucking crap.

Another example of how things may be articulated when digital piracy is described in subpolitical terms is given by Robert (nineteen years old):

> Simon: Do you think of your file sharing as something else than ordinary media consumption?

> Robert: Absolutely! In my daily life I have, like, the opinion that consumption is something disgusting that you should stay away from. I have set principles for my life, among other things that you shouldn't help those large companies who abuse this earth, and that everyone must stop

consuming or else we will perish. And the same goes for . . . even if I would maybe wanna go to the movies, and I can afford going to the movies, I consider it a wrong thing to do. Because then money will go to companies that I don't wish to support. So then I download instead, as a pure act of resistance, so to speak. [. . .] For me, file sharing is a way to exist in society without being forced into this consumption that I wish to avoid.

Simon: Can you understand that it can be a criminal act?

Robert: Yes, of course. It is, isn't it?

Interviewer: But you don't think that makes sense?

Robert: No, no, no [laughing].

The third theme emerging from the interviews—digital piracy as innovation culture—is also based on the idea of digital piracy as a movement supported by enthusiasts, but enthusiasts who are driven by an interest in technology rather than politics. Digital piracy as innovation culture is related to "a small, small group of people that are very technically motivated," so-called members of the scene, or "those driving the rest of the movement forward" (Magnus, twenty-one years old). This small group of people is developing ever more sophisticated ways to circumvent current regulatory frameworks and to find more effective file formats and ways of distribution. Indeed, it was members of such a small group, namely some key users on a Swedish IRC channel, who founded TBP in 2003. At that time, TBP was a meeting place for both hackers and activists who discussed issues of programming as well as continental philosophy, and joined together in different projects (Rydell & Sundberg, 2009).

In sum, the identification of different digital piracy cultures helps to refine the notion of a homogenous group of people sharing some kind of distinct collective identity. The gap between these different cultures is large, and even the digital piracy culture that can be described as political is internally fragmented and ideologically diffuse. Yet, this diversity can be incorporated as a basis for cognitive praxis. In the following sections I argue that cognitive praxis and collective identity can indeed be found among online pirates, despite the heterogeneity that characterizes even the politically organized parts.

Dimensions of Pirate Praxis

Of interest when discussing the organizational dimension is how the heterogeneity of the loosely composited movement is handled and, at the same time,
used to broaden the issue of digital piracy. Referencing statistics on how many
people engage in digital piracy activities is a way to claim legitimacy; this is
occasionally done by, for example, PP. In another example, in one of TBP's
first media appearances in 2003, co-founder Rasmus Fleischer argued that
"there are already millions of people today creating free access, to music and
so on, on the net and no one has really pled the cause of this informal movement of many millions." Later, in interviews with TBP members in 2005, they
carefully emphasized that they are not representing this large and heterogeneous crowd. In practice, the intellectuals of digital piracy have to maintain a
balance between conveying a unified cognitive praxis as a way to exist as
something larger than isolated individual arguments and actions, and empha-
sizing heterogeneity to include different digital piracy cultures, motivations,
and interests. TBP uses this complexity to convey the cosmological dimensions of cognitive praxis. A quote from the back cover of TBP's *Copy Me*
(Kaarto & Fleischer, 2005) illustrates this well: "[t]he perspectives that appear
are both the hacker's, the artist's, the philosopher's and the ordinary file
sharer's [....] From Public Enemy to Friedrich Hayek, from the history of video
games to Michel Foucault, from computer networks to pharmaceutical manu-
facturers." The book is a fragmented collection of various texts such as interviews with movement intellectuals and artists, The Pirate Bay's mocking
public responses to legal threats issued by several large companies, and philosophical texts relating to issues of culture and copyright. TBP burned all their
print copies of the book in a symbolic bonfire on Walpurgis 2007.

The organizational dimension also relates to how the dissemination of
knowledge and ideas is handled within a movement, and to how people are
engaged and new activists are recruited. In the digital piracy movement, the
heterogeneity of the many people engaging in the activity is clear. Potential
new activists, for example, might be found in the sphere of subactivism and
everyday culture. In this process, the technology and its community-building
potential plays an important part. One of the representatives of TBP we interviewed said: "It's an amazing tool! As soon as anything happens, everyone is
gathered. And we can act extremely fast. And even if someone shouldn't be
there, you still never miss out on anything." This focus on participatory and
open forms of communication means that any active forum member becomes

a potential spokesperson or representative of the movement—at least in theory. This can also be interpreted as another way of handling the complexity of representation. Still, in some contexts, the culture of digital piracy is described as very hierarchical and elitist, and is said to exclude people by using complicated technological jargon and codes that are impossible for newcomers or outsiders to understand (Cooper & Harrison, 2001, p. 72). But at least to those who are already "in," spaces such as chats and forums play an important role in fostering the common conscience of the movement.

The technological dimension revolves around the tactics of activists and the actions taken to convey cognitive praxis. In digital piracy, technology and technological development are crucial elements. The most prominent political action related to digital piracy is of course to contribute, by uploading and downloading, to the free flow of culture and information. As discussed above, there is no need for these "activists" to share any collective sense of identity, because what makes the potential movement what it is is the aggregate number of actual digital piracy acts.

Although the everyday practice of actually sharing files is of central importance, there are other actions that are significant to the dissemination of ideas and knowledge related to digital piracy. Some of these actions are similar to the tactics of social movements in history. For example, TBP and PP arranged a number of direct demonstrations and petitions. A rally on International Workers' Day (May 1) in 2004 could have been interpreted as a way to position the organizations' ideas within a social movement heritage, but in this case, pirate demonstrators claimed that the demands of the workers' movement are obsolete. In a text published on several Internet forums, TBP stated that today we must shift the focus of attention toward issues of Internet access and free information as basic human rights:

> The Internet has become a fundamental prerequisite for both work and entertainment—a basic human right like having food for the day or fresh air to breathe. But the access is just as unequally distributed as that to schools or medical services was a hundred years ago.

The use of traditional forms of activism in relation to digital piracy can be seen as a way to draw attention to the cosmological dimensions, the ideas of the potential movement, by making use of methods historically associated with successful social movements. But these tactics are not the main forms of subpolitical practice in the digital piracy movement. Many actions are based mainly in an online environment and built around different networks and projects. In the eyes of the advocates of digital piracy, technology used in the right way can be a tool for decentralizing power. Technology can help the individual resist large-scale industry. There are obvious similarities with the open source and free software movements that promote software with source code that is freely available for others to view, amend, and adapt (DiBona, Ockman, & Stone, 1999; Stallman, 2002), as well as the so-called DiY cultures that consist of people creating things themselves without the aid of paid professionals (McKay, 1998). These are all movements where the very use of certain technologies becomes a political action that can produce a feeling of freedom and autonomy. This is further illustrated by the fact that the restraint of culture in this context can be perceived as an attack on the dignity of the individual: "Pirates are horrified when their connectivity and resources get blocked" (Cooper & Harrison, 2001, p. 86).

In other words, the advocates of digital piracy strive to create a historical project of their own by relating to both the past and the future. The way that they act offensively rather than defensively and their use of humor and symbolism as rhetorical tools are examples of this. In the late 1970s, home taping was blamed for the crisis within the record industry. This led to the "Home taping is killing music (and it's illegal)" campaign in the early 1980s, with the cassette-shaped skull and crossbones logo. The contemporaneous copying movement responded by hijacking the symbol of their antagonists and changing the slogan to "Home taping is killing business (and it's easy)." This took place in an era when the cognitive praxis of today's digital piracy movement was beginning to take shape. The cassette skull became the logotype of TBP, and it is also employed by other actors in the scene. All of this contributes to the construction of collective identity by referring to a common history and symbolism.

The cosmological dimension, finally, revolves around the utopian messages that the movement stands for, what it is that needs to be overcome or transcended (Eyerman & Jamison, 1991). Despite the fact that the movement is ideologically fragmented and heterogeneous, I argue in the following pages that there are in fact a set of common denominators. We can identify, for example, an interesting parallel between the social and the technological elements of digital piracy. The most prominent ideas in the cosmological dimension are the decentralization of power and control, and anti-authoritarianism. These two themes put their mark not only on the interpersonal social relations but also on the technological side of things. For instance, one of the representatives of TBP stated that, to him, digital piracy is first and foremost about technology and its possibilities. In the light of this assertion, it becomes meaningful to describe the cosmological dimension of digital piracy in terms similar to those applied to the hardware of peer-to-peer networks, which are by definition "distributed" in their actual infrastructure (Vaidhyanathan, 2004, p. 17). This is akin to the ethics of "openness, peer review, individual autonomy and communal responsibility" (p. 39) expressed within the preceding hacker culture, the main focus of which is to obtain unauthorized access to various systems through specialist knowledge, skills, and tactics. It also has a clear relation to Castells' (2001) description of an "internet culture" imbued with these ideals and agencies.

Another important aspect of the cosmological dimension is related to the idea that free access to culture and information are basic human rights. The kind of critique of copyright, supported by TBP, is not only about MP3 files or ripped DVDs, but also about many other things such as, for example, the lack of patented and legitimate medications in some developing countries. One of the interviewees from TBP stated: "Partly, we want to broaden the debate to include, maybe, censorship and arts or medical patents and things like that, and connect all of those things. A horizontal widening, you could say, of the debate." Another key cosmological aspect appearing throughout is the criticism of large companies and institutions that use their power to prevent the free flow of culture and information. The same interviewee said: "A world where, like, the companies own any ideas or creativity, that's a very boring world." He said nothing about what ideas or creativity companies might reasonably own. The idea of ownership seems to be interpreted in a very broad sense, bordering on overgeneralization. Similarly, both representatives from TBP expressed rather inexact ideas about "individual freedom." Indeed, it is not always clear whether one should read their argumentation as a radical critique of neoliberal capitalism, or as a defense of such values of "autonomy" and "freedom of choice" that are actually common parts of neoliberal ideology. There is a rather neoliberal idea that what is good for the individual will also be good for others. One of the TBP representatives said:

> It is a kind of egoism that has to include other people, sort of. [. . .] For me to be satisfied, other people around me need to be satisfied too. So, I guess that's the basis of the file sharing movement, maybe. [. . .] Not built on an idea that man has to be in solidarity with others to be good. And like, "you ought to be like this, for moral reasons, and therefore we

should." If we show solidarity towards one another, then it gets better for everyone, kind of. A very primal view of solidarity, you could say.

Digital piracy networks potentially can be used for both politically conservative and radical ends. Again, this may indicate that the phenomenon defies easy categorization along a left-right scale, and/or simply that online pirates are a politically heterogeneous group. In many previous social movements, unity and solidarity within the group played a crucial role. As I have argued in this chapter, digital piracy is clearly more ideologically fragmented and individualistic. This issue was brought forward by one of the interviewees from TBP:

> I can find reasons both for and against file sharing from left-wing as well as right-wing perspectives. I mean, arguments from the left can defend piracy by relating to democracy issues about the importance of everyone getting free access [to information and culture], but they can also be against piracy in order to protect the rights of cultural workers. And on the right-wing side it can, of course, be about protecting the companies, but also about personal freedom and things like that.

This can be interpreted as a strategy by a movement intellectual to deal with the movements' ideological and cosmological differentiation in an inclusive way.

Catching the Third Wave?

Eyerman and Jamison (1998, p. 7) argue that "the collective identity formation that takes place in social movements is a central catalyst of broader changes in values, ideas, and ways of life." In times of change, social movements act as driving forces as well as emergency brakes. The workers' movement in the nineteenth century was a response to certain social transformations. It represented the first wave of modern social movements. The second wave came as a response to postwar societal transformation, and it produced the feminist, civil rights, and environmental movements. Applying this contextual way of looking at social movements, one could ask, what characterizes the social movements that are emerging at our present moment in time? What can be said about the forms of countercultural activism and political participation forty years after 1968, when the second wave of movements has culminated? Are we witnessing a third wave of collective activism, of which the digital piracy movement is an example? And if so, what distinguishes it from, or unites it with, movements of previous eras?

The fact that, from a movement perspective, digital piracy is so loose-knit and heterogeneous is certainly symptomatic of our times. Eyerman and Jamison (1991) claim that today's society is so multifaceted that it is not at all productive to speak of actual movements. The activism of today is described as too limited and part-time to be seen as constituting a new wave of political opposition. Still, from their contextual perspective, it is easy to see how the digital piracy movement springs from noticeable contextual factors at the social and cultural levels—factors summarized by Castells (2001, pp. 36–61) as "the culture of the Internet." This is a culture described in terms of four layers: technomeritocratic culture, hacker culture, the virtual communitarian culture, and entrepreneurial culture.

The first layer is inhabited by a techno-elite with a strong belief in the inherent good of technological development for the progress of society. Among this group, merit is rewarded for contributing to the advancement of the system of networked computers that grows exponentially. As Castells (2001, p. 40) puts it: "The cornerstone of the whole process is the open communication of software." The second layer is composed of hackers with a similar goal of performance, and a common need for sharing and for keeping source codes open. In addition to these two groups of technological innovators, a third layer is populated by virtual communitarians forming communities that give rise to forms of online social organization characterized by "horizontal, free communication" (Castells, 2001, p. 54). The fourth and final layer is made up of entrepreneurs who are forerunners in a process of transformation toward a new economy marked by new rules of production, calculation, and circulation. It is easy to see how the technologically driven and economically disruptive activity of digital piracy, which is clearly based on principles of contribution, networking, and free, horizontal communication of source code, fits into this context.

Although the activism of today may seem to be limited and part-time, the fact is that digital protest occurs on a more than full-time basis. This is because the digital is so large a part of lived everyday practice. It is obvious in the example of the digital piracy movement that, for example, traditional demonstrations and rallies are not the main communicative context. All of the activities related to digital piracy can be seen as examples of how subpolitical participation, innovation, and social movements come into being at the beginning of the twenty-first century. By analyzing digital piracy, we therefore gain a certain insight into how these things work in more general terms in our present day and age; in fact, it is debatable whether co-existing social movements can be understood separately at all. In general, the potential third wave of social movements taking shape today is marked by an emphasis on the interaction between the individual and technology. This is obvious in the digital piracy movement as well as the open source movement, and in the new wave of citizen journalism (Gillmor, 2006; Klein, 1999) and the participatory cultures described by Jenkins (2006) and others. In these cases, the very use of contemporary technologies can contribute to feelings of freedom, autonomy, and empowerment.

· 1 0 ·

A CULTURAL SOCIOLOGY
OF DIGITAL DISRUPTION

*The modern system of publics creates a demanding social phenomeno-
logy. (Warner, 2002a, p. 62)*

This concluding chapter aims to outline the rationale and direction for a cultural sociology of digital disruption. How can we move beyond "vapor theory"
(Lovink, 2002, p. 10)? How can we articulate the net with materiality in a
way that recognizes the embeddednes of social practices? Instead of limiting
academic inquiry to asking "whether or not Google is making us stupid, Facebook is commoditizing our privacy, or Twitter is chopping our attention into
microslices (all good questions)" (Rheingold, 2012, p. 1), how can we contribute to the radically pragmatist project by systematically, theoretically, and
empirically investigating concrete intersections of agency and technology? In
the struggle between socializing and alienating forces in digital culture (Fuchs,
2008, pp. 227–234), how can we best map and analyze the conditions under
which either of these become dominant?

New Noise?

I set out in this book to look for successful tactics for the oppositional use of emergent technologies, for counterpublics taking shape through the interconnection of disruptive spaces. These issues were explored in a set of case studies. The Twitter hashtag as a site of mobilization was explored in chapters 4 and 5, focusing on the WikiLeaks organization and on the Libyan uprising during the Arab Spring. These studies demonstrated that the social and spatial are strongly interlinked in processes of digital disruption. A conclusion of the WikiLeaks case study was that elusive and fluid web spaces, such as those forming around a hashtag, may indeed function as sites of mobilization. This means that they can give rise to shared semiotic and social systems—"cognitive praxis" (Eyerman & Jamison, 1991)—on the basis of which counterpower can be deployed. With the Libyan example, I examined how settlements such as the one forming around the WikiLeaks hashtag interact with other semiotic spaces (e.g., those established by governments, media corporations, organizations, etc.) in complex network relations of power. The case studies also confirmed that hashtags and microblogging can be used to effectively build relatively strong communities that are unified by common ideas, to coordinate protests and disruptive activities online as well as offline, and in several other ways to contribute to balancing discursive power structures.

However, when introducing competing discourses in the analysis, I also found that the real power of the disruptive attempts cannot be taken for granted. There was evidence that oppositional things are being said, and this indicates that social media such as Twitter may be used for deploying disruption. I also found, however, that calls for attention were directed largely toward powerful and corporately controlled news media nodes. Attempts at challenging the symbolic representation of reality may have some sort of impact by spreading throughout a long tail of users, but it is not certain whether a long tail, through aggreggation, adds up to a substantial counterpublic.

In chapter 6, the scope of the discussion was widened to include not only strictly hacktivist contexts, but also a setting that has to do with how symbolic politics in the field of popular culture relates to disruptive skills that are relevant in a more general sense. By looking at the part of online piracy culture that is focused on the creation and distribution of subtitle files, I shed light on processes of status, regulation, and social control in peer production, and concluded that the dual process of collaboration on the one hand and conflict on the other is what constitutes a group as "a concrete, living unit" (Simmel, 1908, p. 77). This highlights the fact that both intergroup and intragroup processes must be analyzed. The multidimensionality of social space (Bourdieu, 1985) means not only that spaces are ordered in relation to each other, but also that agents within spaces are engaged in a symbolic game of status and social regulation.

Chapter 7 explored these issues further by looking at user comments on YouTube, with a focus on the reception of various types of videos. I found that user-created tutorial videos generally were more positively received than other video genres. I explored how media circuits can be formed through the microcontent of YouTube comments, with viewers establishing more or less longstanding contacts with each other based on common interests. While the vastness and fluidity of YouTube makes it problematic to speak of these patterns in terms of community-building, they can be seen as evidence of the existence of affinity spaces (Gee, 2005). Affinity spaces are interactive sites—online or offline—where people come together through common goals, interests, or activities. The analyzed comment threads on how-to videos exemplify this notion. The common endeavor is central, not the homogeneity of the group or the identity of participating individuals.

Chapter 8 analyzed and discussed YouTube comments in relation to discourse produced by "mainstream" or "official" outlets. Using the case of school shootings, I wanted to illustrate how, and under what conditions, comment threads on online videos can function as noise that disrupts prevailing orders of discourse. Referring to the notion of "moral panics" (Cohen, 1972) to describe the reaction sequence found in news reporting as well as search traffic, I turned to McRobbie and Thornton's (1995, p. 564) argument that today's media landscape demands that we "take account of a plurality of reactions, each with their different constituencies, effectivities and modes of discourse." The analyzed comment threads illustrate the process wherein social reality is experienced through language and communication. The reality of school shootings is continuously being defined in these comment threads as users discuss issues of bullying, high school culture, gun control, and racism, while at the same time publically, socially, and emotionally trying to deal with the trauma of these events. The comment thread thus becomes a disruptive space, based on forms of meaning-making that oppose several mainstream and ideological understandings.

In sum, the analyses presented in chapters 4 through 8 led to the following insights:

- Digital media tools and platforms can be used to effectively build strong communities unified by common ideas and focused on disruptive activities that can contribute to balancing discursive power structures.
- Elusive and seemingly fragmented web spaces may function as sites of mobilization.
- In fluid skill zones, people can come together through common goals, interests, or activities to engage in projects where common endeavor is central.
- Disruptive spaces can emerge, based on forms of meaning-making that oppose mainstream and ideological understandings.
- User-created content that aims to disseminate knowledge generally is met with positive responses from other users.
- In media circuits, participants can establish more or less long-standing relations with each other based on shared interests.
- Collaboration is never without conflict, and processes of peer production are characterized by the dual forces of collaboration on the one hand and conflict on the other.
- Studying the potentials and limitations of digital disruption demands taking a highly complex reality into account, with a plurality of modes of interaction and discourse.
- Most importantly, the actual power of the disruptive attempts must never be taken for granted, and the key question is whether, through aggregation, micro-occurrences of disruptive spaces add up to a substantial counterpublic.

An attempt at understanding the translation process between everyday "subactivism" (Bakardjieva, 2009) and the emergence of social movements through the development of cognitive praxis (Eyerman & Jamison, 1991) was made in chapter 9. More study of this is needed however, as is continued retheorization of digital disruption. To claim that digital technology automatically leads to ground-breaking and amazing possibilities for resistance and subversion would be to oversimplify things, not only because there are significant class-based, gendered, and generational differences with regard to access to media and media literacies, but also because the tools are often used in unexpected and innovative ways. Such resourcefulness and creativity come about for a number of reasons that demand constant and renewed investigation if we are to better understand contemporary as well as future forms of political involvement.

A Manifesto for the Analysis of Digital Disruption

Disruption

01. Disruption has to do with politics, defined as the antagonistic dimension which exists in all human relations (Mouffe, 2000, p. 101). Is represents noise—a disturbance in the orderly sequence (Hebdige, 1979, p. 90)—in the present-day context where any social reality is potentially contestable (Carpentier, 2011, p. 40). In digital culture, an increasing number of online socio-cultural spaces are celebrated for being disruptive. Groupings and discourse stemming from these spaces may have the power to circumvent dominant flows of communication, to subvert preferred meanings, and to challenge power structures. An important task for Internet research is to evaluate the conditions under which this power is realized or not.

02. Let us assume that there are *disruptive spaces*. These, then, are emergent online spaces that embody more or less conscious attempts at obstructing or providing an alternative to prevailing discourses. The actual effect and significance of these attempts must always remain an empirical question. We need to assess whether the phenomena we are looking at are in fact challenging hegemony. At best, the disruptive spaces can be novel cultural forms foreboding a dramatic transformation of the social and cultural fabric that enable unprecedented forms of potent rebellion within a number of areas. At worst, they are idealized technodeterministic fantasies failing to account for the continued power of capitalism. Research must be aimed at mapping out the social and symbolic contexts where either of these understandings becomes dominant.

03. The key to realizing the potential of disruptive spaces lies in deploying *emancipatory use of media* (Enzensberger, 1970, p. 26). We need decentralized structures of communication where each receiver is also a transmitter, and where interaction and collective production creates a self-organizing social system that mobilizes the masses to take control of knowledge and power. As researchers of digital disruption, we must look for traces and examples of such media use.

04. Emancipatory media use may be brought into effective action through the formation of *fluid skill zones*—"media circuits" (Lange, 2008; Rouse, 1991); "colonies of enthusiasts" (Rheingold, 1994, p. xxi); "virtual settlements"

(Jones, 1997); "communities of practice" (Wenger, 1998); "affinity spaces" (Gee, 2005); "smart mobs" (Rheingold, 2002); "participatory cultures" (Jenkins, 2006); "networked publics" (Varnelis, 2008); and so on. An important task for Internet studies is to find ways to decide or measure whether such zones are realized, and to contextualize their processes of formation.

05. Disruptive spaces are the latent building blocks of a tentative alternative public sphere. The fluid skill zones may lead to the emergence of a *counterpublic*—where a public is defined as a social imaginary organized by discourse (Warner, 2002b)—based on the production by a "collective intellect" of a distributed discourse in the form of a *cosmopedia* that makes "available to the collective intellect all of the pertinent knowledge available to it at a given moment, but [. . .] also serves as a site of collective discussion, negotiation, and development" (Lévy, 1999, p. 217). It is up to us as researchers to empirically study and theorize the coming into being of such social imaginaries, and to assess the degrees to which democratized and collaborative forms of meaning production are realized.

Power

06. It is under the above conditions that disruptive spaces may be realized and populated by counterpublics "structured by different dispositions or protocols from those that obtain elsewhere in the culture, making different assumptions about what can be said or what goes without saying" (Warner, 2002b, p. 119). But then there is the question of *power*. While the counterpublics may oppose *hegemony* (Gramsci, 1971), there is always "a rarefaction among speaking subjects: none may enter into discourse on a specific subject unless he has satisfied certain conditions or if he is not, from the outset, qualified to do so" (Foucault, 1971, p. 17). This is why some publics "are more likely than others to stand in for *the* public, to frame their address as the universal discussion of the people" (Warner, 2002b, p. 117). As researchers, we must critically approach these issues of domination and subversion.

07. The study of disruptive spaces demands that we adopt a cyber-realist perspective (Kahn & Kellner, 2008; Lovink, 2002; Morozov, 2011, pp. 315–320). This means acknowledging that digital tools and platforms may be used for emancipatory purposes, but also that they may just as well be appropriated by oppressive forces. In digital culture, there is a constant *struggle* between coop-

eration and competition that produces tensions between proprietary space and open space, between networks of domination and networks of liberation (Fuchs, 2008). The researcher must not fall victim to either techno-optimist or techno-pessimist rhetorics. Positioning the analysis within the wider sociological scope of subcultural studies is key to grasping the ways in which digital politics is entangled with ideology and resistance.

08. The continued growth of the Internet and the steady evolution of new gadgets and applications illustrate the importance of McLuhan's (1964) notion of media as constantly evolving environments where new technologies appear all the time. This means that no determined effects can be assumed to follow automatically. Technodeterminism must be avoided at any cost. Uses are always social. For Gramsci (1971), hegemony is a moving equilibrium, and that insight calls for a *constant retheorization* and *critique* of the potential and limitations of digital grassroots engagement. It is the task of Internet researchers to analyze how emergent tools and platforms have provided possibilities for progressive social change and facilitated oppositional cultural and political movements, and also how these same tools have been used for conservative and oppressive ends.

Practice

09. Disruptive spaces exist at the intersection of technology (mediated by protocol at the level of code) and communication (mediated by discourse at the level of language), embedded in social relations (as established via digital media); this *multimodality* must be dealt with when analyzing these spaces. Technological, cultural, and social aspects of the digital cannot be dealt with in isolation from each other, at least not in producing a comprehensive cultural sociology of these settings.

10. Protocol and discourse are structures—rules and resources (Giddens, 1984)—enabling as well as limiting hegemony and resistance. Disruptive spaces are formed in adherence to prevailing discourse/protocol, but if their liberatory potential is realized, they might also function as resistive/counterprotocological forces. Protocol is inextricably entangled with *discourse and language*. Discourse and language, in turn, cannot be studied without addressing also the *spaces of social relations* in which they are used and reproduced. In order to analyze hegemony and resistance, we must take into account classifi-

cations (language/discourse/protocol) as well as the (network) positions occupied by the agents and groups involved.

11. Whether we call our object of study code, protocol, discourse, or language, the place to look for it to come into being is in *practice*. The only way to comprehensively deal with technological, cultural, and social aspects of the Internet without remaining in a purely philosophical domain is to empirically analyze what actually happens. This is a basic tenet of cultural sociology: Life in social spaces must be studied through the practice where, according to Bourdieu (1984, p. 101), habitus and capital is put into play in various fields. This practice is highly textual and thus readable.

Moving Equilibrium

While I have presented in this book examples in which digital disruption has been deployed more or less successfully, I have underlined all along the importance of retaining a critical perspective. My main argument is not that digital disruption works, but that it *may* work under certain circumstances—"networks, by their mere existence, are not liberating" (Galloway & Thacker, 2007, p. 5). There is a pressing need for more knowledge on how grassroots digital politics works, when it works. Ultimately, this book is a plea to take Internet studies into a new era of systematic empirical inquiry of the processes by which the power of the good examples might be harnessed toward a more substantial transformation of the public.

As academics, we must engage in the continued retheorization of digital disruption. Also, we must work harder to understand how the attempts at disruption sit within the wider framework of "communicative capitalism" (Dean, 2009). While hegemony *might* be disrupted, the massive circulation of content in dense networks through "myriad intense exchanges" may in fact relieve "top-level actors (corporate, institutional, and governmental) from the obligation to answer" (Dean, 2009, p. 21). Kluitenberg (2011, pp. 14–15) writes:

> While amateur practice still challenges established hierarchies of professional knowledge production, and with that the definition of what constitutes valuable knowledge, it has now become strangely encapsulated by professional market machines and monetising mechanisms.

There is no significant difference any longer between the online and the offline, between cyberspace and meatspace. If the digital were one homogenous tool, related to a singular set of practices for achieving a certain number of ends, we could aspire to measure its efficiency in order to promote democracy. But the digital is reality, and it is society. How to measure the efficiency of such abstract constructs? Mosco (2004, p. 19) writes:

> [T]he real power of new technologies does not appear during their mythic period, when they are hailed for their ability to bring world peace, renew communities, or end scarcity, history, geography, or politics; rather, their social impact is greatest when technologies become banal—when they literally (as in the case of electricity) or figuratively withdraw into the woodwork. [...] Indeed, it was not until we stopped looking at electricity as a discrete wonder and began to see it as a contributor to all the other forces in society that it became an extraordinary force.

It is time now to demystify the digital. More than a decade into the twenty-first century, we must finally shake the imagery of VR-helmets as well as the illusion of disembodied and placeless cyberspace surfing. Understanding the digital is not understanding a "medium" in the sense of a radio or a telephone. Rather, it is grasping the very fabric and architecture of the present-day social. There are no all-embracing answers: "The quest for 'universals of communication' ought to make us shudder" (Deleuze, 1995, p. 175).

Rewind: Objective vs. Subjective Culture

Revisiting Simmel's *The Philosophy of Money* (1900) we find as a key theme in his analysis of the late nineteenth-century capitalist economy the struggle between objective and subjective culture. He writes that "the contents of the world"—e.g., media technologies—"are completely neutral, but at one point or another they become coloured by the will" (Simmel, 1900, p. 430). Without human desires, emotions, and ideas utilizing "the available possibilities of objects" (p. 447), these objects will not be cultivated—their value will not be increased "beyond the performance of their natural constitution" (p. 447). Culture is about shaping objects, as digital culture is about shaping technology. This is done, however, under specific conditions.

Simmel argued that "the things that determine and surround our lives, such as tools, means of transport, the products of science, technology and art, are extremely refined" (p. 448). Much like what often is said about digital culture, he wrote that "we have a large number of refinements, subtleties and individual modes of expression" (p. 448). However, like the current critics of overly celebratory perspectives on the new forms of communication, Simmel felt that the new modes of expression were "less correct, less dignified and more trivial"; he claimed they were "more superficial, less interesting and less serious" (p. 448).

When the technologies are more refined than their realized uses, we may witness "a real triumph of objective culture" (Simmel, 1900, p. 449). In the capitalist economy, of which digital networks and social media are part (Castells, 1996; Dean, 2009; Fuchs, 2011; Mosco, 1996),

> exchange relations become increasingly complicated and mediated with the result that the economy necessarily estabishes more and more relationships and obligations *that are not directly reciprocal*. It is obvious how much this objectifies the whole character of transactions and how subjectivity is destroyed and transposed into cool reserve and anonymous objectivity once so many intermediate stages are introduced between the producer and the customer that they lose sight of each other. (Simmel, 1900, p. 457)

Ultimately, what determines whether digital disruption works or not has to do with the "moving equilibrium" of hegemony (Gramsci, 1971) and the "occasional greater weight" (Simmel, 1900, p. 463) of subjective or objective culture—the tug of war between socializing and alienating cyberculture (Fuchs, 2008, pp. 327–330). In the words of Castells (2007, p. 250), the challenge consists in "building networks of meaning in opposition to networks of instrumentality."

Fast Forward: Transgressing into Hybrid Space

In the digital network, the triumph of objective culture happens when the new infrastructure—which may invigorate marginal actors in social, political, cultural, or artistic settings—leads to an insulation that is hard to transcend (Kluitenberg, 2011, p. 9). While the network made it possible for social movements to escape "their confinement in the fragmented space of places" through seizing "the global space of flows" (Castells, 2007, p. 250), the new forms of counterpower risk being encapsulated in the digital. As underlined in de Certeau's (1984, p. xix) definition of "tactics," a disruptive space "insinuates itself into the other's place fragmentarily, without taking it over in its entirety, without being able to keep it at a distance."

In communicative capitalism (Dean, 2009), potentially disruptive forces may be displaced and rendered harmless as they become contained in "the circuits of drive" (Dean, 2010). In objective culture, communicative exchanges are capitalized and commodified in ways that may imply "the destruction of the political" (Kluitenberg, 2011, p. 10). For subjective culture to break through this containment, what is needed is a "transgression into public" (Kluitenberg, 2011, p. 10). This transgression, however, does not entail moving from one clear-cut domain into another. Rather, it is about navigating emerging forms of hybrid space. Castells (2007, p. 249) writes that disruptive spaces are "not originated by technology, they use technology. But technology is not simply a tool, it is a medium, it is a social construction, with its own implications." Materialities, bodies, and places of the present adhere, as a consequence of their media-saturation, to a hybridized logic.

> Hybrid Space offers a conception of space as a layered construct where media and embodied spaces no longer are considered to exist in parallel or in opposition, but rather coexist as heterogenous elements and flows superimposed upon each other as sedimentary layers within the same spatial confine. (Castells, 2007, p. 11)

At the core of it all, the analysis of digital disruption—whether it is focused on the mobilization of oppressed populations into streets and squares, the empowerment of fan cultures in the pop cultural sphere of semiotic politics, or the creation of alternative discourses for understanding social reality—is about analyzing twenty-first-century social movements in all their fluidity and fragmentation. Melucci (1989, p. 75) writes of new social movements as networks of sociocultural innovators that challenge dominant cultural codes while developing new "models of behavior and social relationships that enter into everyday life" in the form of what might be called subpolitics (Beck, 1997) or subactivism (Bakardjieva, 2009). The future study of disruptive spaces must not only take into account the overtly and traditionally "political" forms of participation, but also consider how the "new horizontal networking practices can be incorporated into more everyday forms of social, economic, and political life" (Juris, 2005, p. 205). Disruptive spaces and their interconnections are rhizomatic (Deleuze & Guattari, 1987), distributed, branching, emergent, constantly fusing together, and hiving off. As Juris (2005, p. 199) emphasizes:

> [...] it is important to consider how such contradictory processes are actually generated in practice through concrete networking politics, which are always entangled within complex relationships of power rendered visible through long-term ethnographic research.

Disruptive spaces can be constituted as spaces without being hybrid. They can exist online, in the virtual, confined and contained within the circuits of drive. The meanings that they produce can be disruptive without the spaces transgressing into the public. Oppositional and subversive discourse may be generated and circulated within these same circuits. But in order for disruptive spaces to actually make a difference, and not just as sources of inspiration, identity, and mutual support in electronic isolation, they must be hybrid. Advocates of tactical media are now calling for a return to the streets; the network itself, through ubiquitous and wirelessly dispersed technologies, is already there.

WORKS CITED

Adorno, T. W., and M. Horkheimer. (1947). *Dialectic of enlightenment.* London: Verso.

Alexander, B., and A. Levine. (2008). "Web 2.0 storytelling: Emergence of a new genre." *EDUCAUSE Review* 43: 1–8.

Althusser, L. (1969). *For Marx.* London: Verso.

Anderson, C. (2006). *The long tail: How endless choice is creating unlimited demand.* London: Random House Business.

Anderson, L. (2011). "Demystifying the Arab Spring." *Foreign Affairs* 90(3): 2–7.

Anstead, N., and A. Chadwick. (2008). "Parties, election campaigning, and the Internet: Toward a comparative institutional approach." In Chadwick, A., and P. Howard (Eds.), *The Routledge handbook of Internet politics* (pp. 56–71). London: Routledge.

Bakardjieva, M. (2009). "Subactivism: Lifeworld and politics in the age of the Internet." *The Information Society* 25(2): 91–104.

Barabási, A.-L. (2002). *Linked: The new science of networks.* Cambridge, MA: Perseus Books.

Barnard-Wills, D. (2011). "'This is not a cyber war, it's a ... ?': Wikileaks, Anonymous and the politics of hegemony." *International Journal of Cyber Warfare and Terrorism* 1(1): 13–23.

Baron, N. S. (2005). "The future of written culture: Envisioning language in the new millennium." *Ibérica* 9: 7–31.

Barthes, R. (1972). *Mythologies.* London: Cape.

Bastian, M., S. Heymann et al. (2009). "Gephi: An open source software for exploring and manipulating networks." Paper presented at the AAAI Conference on Weblogs and Social Media, San Jose, California.

Baudrillard, J. (1981). *For a critique of the political economy of the sign.* St. Louis, MO: Telos Press.

Beck, U. (1997). *The reinvention of politics: Rethinking modernity in the global social order.* Cambridge, UK: Polity Press.

Benkler, Y. (2006). *The wealth of networks: How social production transforms markets and freedom.* New Haven, CT: Yale University Press.

Bennett, A., and K. Kahn-Harris. (2004). *After subculture: Critical studies in contemporary youth culture.* New York: Palgrave.

Berelson, B. (1952). *Content analysis in communication research.* New York: Hafner.

Bernhardsson, S., L. E. C. Da Rocha et al. (2010). "Size-dependent word frequencies and translational invariance of books." *Physica A: Statistical Mechanics and Its Applications* 389(2): 330–341.

Boehlert, E. (2009). *Bloggers on the bus: How the Internet changed politics and the press.* New York: Free Press.

Bond, R. (1999). "Links, frames, meta-tags and trolls." *International Review of Law, Computers & Technology* 13: 317–323.

Bourdieu, P. (1977a). "The economics of linguistic exchanges." *Social Science Information* 16: 145–668.

———. (1977b). *Outline of a theory of practice.* New York: Cambridge University Press.

———. (1984). *Distinction: A social critique of the judgement of taste.* Cambridge, MA: Harvard University Press.

———. (1985). "The social space and the genesis of groups." *Theory and Society* 14(6): 723–744.

———. (1989). "Social space and symbolic power." *Sociological Theory* 7(1): 14–25.

———. (1990). *The logic of practice.* Cambridge, UK: Polity Press.

———. (1991). *Language and symbolic power.* Cambridge, UK: Polity Press.

———. (2000). *Pascalian meditations.* Cambridge, UK: Polity Press.

Brady, H. E., and D. Collier. (2004). *Rethinking social inquiry: Diverse tools, shared standards.* Lanham, MD: Rowman & Littlefield.

Broder, A., R. Kumar et al. (2000). "Graph structure in the web." *Computer Networks* 33(1): 309–320.

Bruns, A. (2008). *Blogs, Wikipedia, Second Life, and beyond: From production to produsage.* New York: Peter Lang.

Bruns, A., and J. Burgess. (2011). "The use of Twitter hashtags in the formation of ad hoc publics." Paper presented at the European Consortium for Political Research Conference, Reykjavik, Iceland.

Bruns, A., J. Burgess et al. (2011). "Mapping the Australian networked public sphere." *Social Science Computer Review* 29(3): 277–287.

Burgess, J., and J. Green. (2009). *YouTube: Online video and participatory culture.* Cambridge, UK: Polity Press.

Burns, A., and B. Eltham. (2009). "Twitter free Iran: An evaluation of Twitter's role in public diplomacy and information operations in Iran's 2009 election crisis." In Papandrea, F., and M. Armstrong (Eds.), *Record of the Communications Policy & Research Forum 2009* (pp. 298–310). Sydney: Network Insight Institute.

Burns, R., and C. Crawford. (1999). "School shootings, the media, and public fear: Ingredients for a moral panic." *Crime, Law and Social Change* 32: 147–168.

Burr, V. (2003). *Social constructionism*. London: Routledge.

Callon, M., J. Courtial et al. (1991). "Co-word analysis as a tool for describing the network of interactions between basic and technological research: The case of polymer chemistry." *Scientometrics* 22(1): 155–205.

Carpentier, N. (2011). *Media and participation: A site of ideological-democratic struggle*. Bristol, UK: Intellect Books.

Castells, M. (1996). *The information age: Economy, society and culture*, vol. 1: *The rise of the network society*. Malden, MA: Blackwell.

———. (2001). *The Internet galaxy: Reflections on the Internet, business and society*. Oxford, UK: Oxford University Press.

———. (2007). "Communication, power and counter-power in the network society." *International Journal of Communication* 1(1): 238–266.

———. (2009). *Communication power*. Oxford, UK: Oxford University Press.

Cattuto, C., V. Loreto et al. (2007). "Semiotic dynamics and collaborative tagging." *Proceedings of the National Academy of Sciences* 104: 1461–1464.

Chaney, D. (2004). "Fragmented culture and subcultures." In Bennett, A., and K. Kahn-Harris (Eds.), *After subculture: Critical studies in contemporary youth culture* (pp. 36–48). New York: Palgrave Macmillan.

Cheng, X., C. Dale et al. (2008). Statistics and social network of YouTube videos. *Proceedings of the 16th International Workshop on Quality of Service, Enschede, Netherlands*: 229–238.

Christakis, N., and J. Fowler. (2010). *Connected: The amazing power of social networks and how they shape our lives*. New York: Little, Brown & Company.

Christensen, H. S. (2011). "Political activities on the Internet: Slacktivism or political participation by other means?" *First Monday* 16(2).

Clarke, J., S. Hall et al. (1975). "Subcultures, cultures and class." In Hall, S., and T. Jefferson (Eds.), *Resistance through rituals: Youth subcultures in post-war Britain* (pp. 9–74). London: Hutchinson.

Coffey, B., and S. Woolworth (2004). "'Destroy the scum, and then neuter their families': The web forum as a vehicle for community discourse?" *Social Science Journal* 41: 1–14.

Cohen, S. (1972). *Folk devils and moral panics: The creation of the mods and rockers*. London: Blackwell.

Cohen, S., and J. Young. (1973). *The manufacture of news: Social problems, deviance and the mass media*. London: Constable.

Cooper, J., and D. M. Harrison. (2001). "The social organization of audio piracy on the Internet." *Media, Culture and Society* 23: 71–89.

Crystal, D. (2001). *Language and the Internet*. New York: Cambridge University Press.

de Certeau, M. (1984). *The practice of everyday life*. Berkeley: University of California Press.

De Nooy, W., A. Mrvar et al. (2011). *Exploratory social network analysis with Pajek*. New York: Cambridge University Press.

Dean, J. (2009). *Democracy and other neoliberal fantasies: Communicative capitalism & left politics*. Durham, NC: Duke University Press.

———. (2010). *Blog theory: Feedback and capture in the circuits of drive*. Cambridge, UK: Polity Press.

Dean, J., J. W. Anderson et al. (2006). *Reformatting politics: Information technology and global civil society*. New York: Routledge.

Deerwester, S., S. T. Dumais et al. (1990). "Indexing by latent semantic analysis." *Journal of the American Society for Information Science* 41(6): 391–407.

Deleuze, G. (1995). "Control and becoming." In *Negotiations: 1972–1990* (M. Joughin, Trans.) (pp.169–176). New York: Columbia University Press.

Deleuze, G., and F. Guattari. (1987). *A thousand plateaus: Capitalism and schizophrenia.* Minneapolis: University of Minnesota Press.

DiBona, C., S. Ockman et al. (1999). *Open sources: Voices from the open source revolution.* London: O'Reilly.

Donath, J. S. (1999). "Identity and deception in the virtual community." In Smith, M. A., and P. Kollock (Eds.), *Communities in cyberspace* (pp. 29–59). New York: Routledge.

Doppelt, G. (2001). "What sort of ethics does technology require?" *Journal of Ethics* 5(2): 155–175.

Downey, J., and N. Fenton. (2003). "New media, counter publicity and the public sphere." *New Media & Society* 5(2): 185.

Drotner, K. (1999). "Dangerous media? Panic discourses and dilemmas of modernity." *Paedagogica Historica* 35: 593–619.

Durkheim, É. (1895). *The rules of sociological method.* Chicago: Collier-Macmillan.

Eco, U. (1976). *A theory of semiotics.* Bloomington: Indiana University Press.

Ellison, N. B., and D. Boyd. (2007). "Social network sites: Definition, history, and scholarship." *Journal of Computer-Mediated Communication* 13: 210–230.

Ellson, J., E. Gansner et al. (2002). "Graphviz—open source graph drawing tools." In Mutzel, P., M. Jünger, and S. Leipert (Eds.), *Graph drawing* (pp. 594–597). Berlin and Heidelberg: Springer.

Enzensberger, H. M. (1970). "Constituents of a theory of the media." *New Left Review* 1: 64.

Erickson, T. (1997). "Social interaction on the Net: Virtual community as participatory." *Proceedings of the 30th Hawaii International Conference on System Sciences: Digital Documents* 6: 13–21.

Eyerman, R., and A. Jamison. (1991). *Social movements: A cognitive approach.* University Park: Pennsylvania State University Press.

———. (1998). *Music and social movements: Mobilizing traditions in the twentieth century.* Cambridge, UK: Cambridge University Press.

Fairclough, N. (1989). *Language and power.* London: Longman.

———. (1995). *Critical discourse analysis: The critical study of language.* London: Longman.

Fiske, J. (1989). *Understanding popular culture.* Boston: Unwin Hyman.

Flick, U. (1992). "Triangulation revisited: Strategy of validation or alternative?" *Journal for the Theory of Social Behaviour* 22(2): 175–197.

Foucault, M. (1971). "Orders of discourse." *Social Science Information* 10: 7–30.

Fraser, N. (1990). "Rethinking the public sphere: A contribution to the critique of actually existing democracy." *Social Text* (25/26): 56–80.

Fuchs, C. (2008). *Internet and society: Social theory in the information age.* New York: Routledge.

———. (2011). *Foundations of critical media and information studies.* New York: Routledge.

Galloway, A. R. (2004). *Protocol: How control exists after decentralization.* Cambridge, MA: MIT Press.

Galloway, A. R., and E. Thacker. (2007). *The exploit: A theory of networks.* Minneapolis: University of Minnesota Press.

Garcia, D., and G. Lovink. (1997). "The ABC of tactical media." *Nettime* (16 MAY).

Gauntlett, D. (2011). *Making is connecting: The social meaning of creativity, from DIY and knitting to YouTube and Web 2.0.* Cambridge, UK: Polity Press.

Gee, J. P. (2005). "Semiotic social spaces and affinity spaces: From the age of mythology to today's schools." In Barton, D., and K. Tusting (Eds.), *Beyond communities of practice: Language, power and social context* (pp. 214–232). New York: Cambridge University Press.

Gelder, K. (2005). *The subcultures reader.* London: Routledge.

Gergen, K. (1985). "The social constructionist movement in modern social psychology." *American Psychologist* 40(3): 266–275.

Gessen, K. (2012). *Occupy!: Scenes from occupied America.* London: Verso.

Gibson, R., A. Römmele et al. (2003). "German parties and Internet campaigning in the 2002 federal election." *German Politics* 12(1): 79–108.

Giddens, A. (1984). *The constitution of society: Outline of the theory of structuration.* Cambridge, UK: Polity Press.

Gillmor, D. (2006). *We the media: Grassroots journalism by the people, for the people.* Beijing: O'Reilly.

Glaser, B. G. (1965). "The constant comparative method of qualitative analysis." *Social Problems* 12: 436–445.

———. (1978). *Theoretical sensitivity: Advances in the methodology of grounded theory.* Mill Valley, CA: Sociology Press.

Glaser, B. G., and A. L. Strauss. (1967). *The discovery of grounded theory: Strategies for qualitative research.* Chicago: Aldine.

Golder, S. A., and M. W. Macy. (2011). "Diurnal and seasonal mood vary with work, sleep, and daylength across diverse cultures." *Science* 333(6051): 1878–1881.

Goode, E., and N. Ben-Yehuda. (1994). *Moral panics: The social construction of deviance.* Cambridge, UK: Blackwell.

———. (2006). "Moral panics: An introduction." In Critcher, C. (Ed.), *Critical readings: Moral panics and the media* (pp. 50–59). Maidenhead, UK: Open University Press.

Gordon, M. M. (1947). "The concept of the sub-culture and its application." *Social Forces* 26(1): 40–42.

Gramsci, A. (1971). *Selections from the prison notebooks of Antonio Gramsci.* London: Lawrence and Wishart.

Grossman, L. (2009). "Iran protests: Twitter, the medium of the movement." *Time* (17 JUNE).

Grusin, R. (2009). "YouTube at the end of new media." In Snickars, P., and P. Vonderau (Eds.), *The YouTube reader* (pp. 60–67). Stockholm: National Library of Sweden.

Habermas, J. (1989). *The structural transformation of the public sphere: An inquiry into a category of bourgeois society.* Cambridge, UK: Polity Press.

Hall, S. (1997). "The work of representation." In *Representation: Cultural representations and signifying practices* (pp. 13–74). London: Sage.

Hall, S., C. Critcher et al. (1978). *Policing the crisis: Mugging, the state, and law and order.* London: Macmillan.

Hands, J. (2011). *@ is for activism: Dissent, resistance and rebellion in a digital culture.* London: Pluto.

Harfoush, R. (2009). *Yes we did!: An inside look at how social media built the Obama brand.* Berkeley, CA: New Riders.

Hebdige, D. (1979). *Subculture: The meaning of style*. London: Routledge.

Herring, S., K. Job-Sluder et al. (2002). "Searching for safety online: Managing 'trolling' in a feminist forum." *The Information Society* 18: 371–384.

Herrmann, A., and L. Cronqvist. (2006). "Contradictions in qualitative comparative analysis (QCA): Ways out of the dilemma." EUI Working Papers, SPS 2006/06. Florence, Italy: European University Institute.

Herz, J. C. (2002). "Harnessing the hive: How online games drive networked innovation." *Release 1.0* 20: 1–22.

Holland, N. (1996). "The Internet regression." *The Psychology of Cyberspace* 1.0 (January). Retrieved from http://users.rider.edu/~suler/psycyber/holland.html

Hooghe, M., and W. Teepe. (2007). "Party profiles on the web: An analysis of the log files of non-partisan interactive political internet sites in the 2003 and 2004 election campaigns in Belgium." *New Media & Society* 9(6): 965.

Ito, M. (2008). "Introduction." In Varnelis, K. (Ed.), *Networked publics* (pp. 1–14). Cambridge, MA: MIT Press.

Jansen, F. (2010). "Digital activism in the Middle East: Mapping issue networks in Egypt, Iran, Syria and Tunisia." *Knowledge Management for Development Journal* 6(1): 37–52.

Jenkins, H. (2006). *Convergence culture: Where old and new media collide*. New York: New York University Press.

Jenkins, H., K. Clinton et al. (2009). *Confronting the challenges of participatory culture: Media education for the 21st century*. Cambridge, MA: MIT Press.

Jenks, C. (2005). *Subculture: The fragmentation of the social*. London: Sage.

Jensen, K. B. (2002). *The complementarity of qualitative and quantitative methodologies in media and communication research*. London: Routledge.

Jick, T. D. (1979). "Mixing qualitative and quantitative methods: Triangulation in action." *Administrative Science Quarterly* 24(4): 602–611.

Jones, G. M., and B. B. Schieffelin. (2009). "Talking text and talking back: 'My BFF Jill' from boob tube to YouTube." *Journal of Computer-Mediated Communication* 14: 1050–1079.

Jones, Q. (1997). "Virtual communities, virtual settlements & cyberarchaeology: A theoretical outline." *Journal of Computer Mediated Communication* 3: 35–49.

Jones, S. (1994). "Understanding community in the information age." In *CyberSociety: Computer-mediated communication and community* (pp. 10–35). Thousand Oaks, CA: Sage.

Joshi, A. K. (1991). "Natural language processing." *Science* 253(5025): 1242.

Juris, J. S. (2005). "The new digital media and activist networking within anti-corporate globalization movements." *Annals of the American Academy of Political and Social Science* 597(1): 189–208.

Kaarto, M., and R. Fleischer. (2005). *Copy me: Samlade texter från Piratbyrån*. Stockholm: Rohnin.

Kahn, R., and D. Kellner. (2008). "Technopolitics, blogs, and emergent media ecologies: A critical/reconstructive approach." In Hawk, B., D. M. Rieder, and O. Oviedo (Eds.), *Small tech: The culture of digital tools* (pp. 22–37). Minneapolis: University of Minnesota Press.

Kellner, D. (1996). "Baudrillard: A new McLuhan?" *Illuminations* 127(7). Retrieved from http://www.uta.edu/huma/illuminations/kell26.htm.

Khonsari, K. K., Z. A. Nayeri et al. (2010). "Social network analysis of Iran's green movement opposition groups using Twitter." Paper presented at the International Conference on Advances in Social Networks Analysis and Mining, Odense, Denmark.

Klein, H. K. (1999). "Tocqueville in cyberspace: Using the Internet for citizen associations." *The Information Society* 15: 213–220.

Klein, N. (2000). *No logo: Taking aim at the brand bullies.* London: Flamingo.

Kluitenberg, E. (2011). *Legacies of tactical media: The tactics of cccupation from Tompkins Square to Tahrir.* Amsterdam: Institute of Network Cultures.

Krippendorff, K. (1980). *Content analysis: An introduction to its methodology.* London: Sage.

Kroski, E. (2005). "The hive mind: Folksonomies and user-based tagging." Retrieved from http://infotangle.blogsome.com/2005/12/07/thehive-mind-folksonomies-and-user-based-tagging/

Kuran, T. (1989). "Sparks and prairie fires: A theory of unanticipated political revolution." *Public Choice* 61(1): 41–74.

Laclau, E., and C. Mouffe. (1985). *Hegemony and socialist strategy.* London: Verso.

Lange, P. G. (2008). "Publicly private and privately public: Social networking on YouTube." *Journal of Computer-Mediated Communication* 13: 361–380.

Lanier, J. (2010). *You are not a gadget: A manifesto.* New York: Alfred A. Knopf.

Lee, A. M. C. (1945). "Levels of culture as levels of social generalization." *American Sociological Review* 10(4): 485–495.

Lefebvre, H. (1971). *Everyday life in the modern world.* New York: Harper and Row.

Lefebvre, H———. (1974). *The production of space.* Oxford, UK: Basil Blackwell.

Lentricchia, F., and A. DuBois. (2003). *Close reading: The reader.* Durham, NC: Duke University Press.

Lévy, P. (1999). *Collective intelligence: Mankind's emerging world in cyberspace.* Cambridge, MA: Perseus Books.

Lindgren, S. (2009). "Unga fildelningskulturer." In *Ungdomskulturer* (pp. 118–131). Malmö, Sweden: Gleerups.

———. (2011). "YouTube gunmen? Mapping participatory media discourse on school shooting videos." *Media, Culture & Society* 33: 123–136.

———. (2012). "'It took me about half an hour, but I did it!' Media circuits and affinity spaces around how-to videos on YouTube." *European Journal of Communication* 27(2): 152–170.

Lindgren, S., and J. Linde. (2012). "The subpolitics of online piracy: A Swedish case study." *Convergence: The International Journal of Research into New Media Technologies* 18: 121–125.

Lindgren, S., and R. Lundström. (2011). "Pirate culture and hacktivist mobilization: The cultural and social protocols of# WikiLeaks on Twitter." *New Media & Society* 13(6): 999–1018.

Lindgren, S., and F. Palm. (2011). *Textometrica: Service package for text analysis.* Umeå, Sweden: HUMlab.

Liu, G. Z. (1999). "Virtual community presence in Internet relay chatting." *Journal of Computer-Mediated Communication* 5(1). Retrieved from http://jcmc.indiana.edu/vol5/issue1/liu.htm.

Lovink, G. (2002). *Dark fiber: Tracking critical Internet culture.* Cambridge, MA: MIT Press.

———. (2005). *The principle of notworking: Concepts in critical Internet culture.* Amsterdam: Amsterdam University Press.

———. (2012). *Networks without a cause: A critique of social media.* Cambridge, UK: Polity Press.

Lovink, G., and S. Niederer. (2008). *Video vortex reader: Responses to Youtube.* Amsterdam: Institute of Network Cultures.

Lovink, G., N. Rossiter et al. (2009). "The digital given: 10 Web 2.0 theses." *Fibreculture* 14. Retrieved from http://fourteen.fibreculturejournal.org/fcj-096-the-digital-given-10-web-2-0-theses/

Maguire, B., G. A. Weatherby et al. (2002). "Network news coverage of school shootings." *The Social Science Journal* 39: 465–470.

Malcolm X. (1963/2006). "Message to the grassroots." In Rudnick, L. P., J. E. Smith, and R. L. Rubin (Eds.), *American identities: An introductory textbook* (pp. 119–125). Malden, MA: Blackwell.

Manning, C. D., H. Schütze et al. (1999). *Foundations of statistical natural language processing.* Cambridge, MA: MIT Press.

Mason, P. (2012). *Why it's kicking off everywhere: The new global revolutions.* London: Verso.

McCaughey, M., and M. D. Ayers. (2003). *Cyberactivism: Online activism in theory and practice.* New York: Routledge.

McKay, G. (1998). *DiY culture: Party and protest in nineties' Britain.* London: Verso.

McLuhan, M. (1964). *Understanding media: The extensions of man.* London: Routledge.

McRobbie, A., and S. L. Thornton. (1995). "Rethinking 'moral panic' for multi-mediated social worlds." *British Journal of Sociology* 46: 559–574.

Melucci, A. (1989). *Nomads of the present: Social movements and individual needs in contemporary society.* London: Hutchinson Radius.

———. (1996). *Challenging codes: Collective action in the information age.* Cambridge, UK: Cambridge University Press.

Mises, L. v. (1960). *Epistemological problems of economics.* Princeton, NJ: D. Van Nostrand.

Moretti, F. (2005). *Graphs, maps, trees: Abstract models for a literary history.* New York: Verso Books.

Morozov, E. (2011). *The net delusion: The dark side of Internet freedom.* New York: Public Affairs.

Mosco, V. (1996). *The political economy of communication: Rethinking and renewal.* London: Sage.

———. (2004). *The digital sublime: Myth, power, and cyberspace.* Cambridge, MA: MIT Press.

Mouffe, C. (2000). *The democratic paradox.* London: Verso.

Muggleton, D., and R. Weinzierl. (2003). *The post-subcultures reader.* Oxford, UK: Berg.

Müller, E. (2009). "Where quality matters: Discourses of the art of making a YouTube video." In Snickars, P., and P. Vonderau (Eds.), *The YouTube reader* (pp. 126–139). Stockholm: National Library of Sweden.

Munteanu, I., and A. Mungiu-Pippidi. (2009). "Moldova's 'Twitter revolution.'" *Journal of Democracy* 20(3): 136–142.

Neuendorf, K. A. (2002). *The content analysis guidebook.* London: Sage.

O'Reilly, T. (2007). "What is Web 2.0: Design patterns and business models for the next generation of software." Retrieved from http://www.oreilly.com/web2/archive/what-is-web-20.html.

Osareh, F. (1996). "Bibliometrics, citation analysis and co-citation analysis: A review of the literature." *Libri* 46: 149–158, 217–225.

Paolillo, J. C. (2008). "Structure and network in the YouTube core." *Proceedings of the 41st Annual Hawaii International Conference on System Sciences* (HICSS 2008): 156–156.

Pearson, G. (1983). *Hooligan: A history of respectable fears.* London: Macmillan.

Peirce, C. S. (1932). *Collected papers of Charles Sanders Peirce*, vol. 2: *Elements of logic*. Cambridge, MA: Belknap Press of Harvard University Press.

Ragin, C. C. (2000). *Fuzzy-set social science*. Chicago: University of Chicago Press.

Raley, R. (2009). *Tactical media*. Minneapolis: University of Minnesota Press.

Rehn, A. (2004). "The politics of contraband: The honor economies of the warez scene." *Journal of Socio-Economics* 33: 359–374.

Rheingold, H. (1993). *The virtual community: Homesteading on the electronic frontier*. London: Secker & Warburg.

———. (1994). *The virtual community: Finding connection in a computerized world*. London: Secker & Warburg.

———. (2002). *Smart mobs: The next social revolution*. Cambridge, MA: Perseus.

———. (2012). *Net smart: How to thrive online*. Cambridge, MA: MIT Press.

Ritzer, G., and N. Jurgenson. (2010). "Production, consumption, prosumption: The nature of capitalism in the age of the digital 'prosumer.'" *Journal of Consumer Culture* 10: 13–36.

Rojek, C. (2005). "P2P leisure exchange: Net banditry and the policing of intellectual property." *Leisure Studies* 24: 357–369.

Rouse, R. (1991). "Mexican migration and the social space of postmodernism." *Diaspora: A Journal of Transnational Studies* 1: 8–23.

Rydell, A., and S. Sundberg. (2009). *Piraterna: Framgångssagan om Piratpartiet, Pirate Bay och Piratbyrån*. Stockholm: Ordfront.

Saussure, F. d. (1960). *Course in general linguistics*. London: Owen.

Sedereviciute, K., and C. Valentini. (2011). "Towards a more holistic stakeholder analysis approach: Mapping known and undiscovered stakeholders from social media." *International Journal of Strategic Communication* 5(4): 221–239.

Sharma, A. S., and M. Elidrisi. (2008). "Classification of multi-media content (videos on YouTube) using tags and focal points." Unpublished manuscript.

Shirky, C. (2008). *Here comes everybody: The power of organizing without organizations*. New York: Penguin.

Simmel, G. (1900). *The philosophy of money*. London: Routledge.

———. (1908). "Conflict." In *On individuality and social forms: Selected writings* (pp. 70–95). Chicago: University of Chicago Press.

Skinner, J. (2011). "Social media and revolution: The Arab Spring and the Occupy movement as seen through three information studies paradigms." *Sprouts: Working Papers on Information Systems* 11(169).

Snickars, P., and P. Vonderau. (2009). *The YouTube reader*. Stockholm: National Library of Sweden.

Stallman, R. M. (2002). *Free software, free society: Selected essays of Richard M. Stallman*. Boston: GNU Press.

Suler, J. (2004). "The online disinhibition effect." *CyberPsychology & Behavior* 7: 321–326.

Swedberg, R. (1990). "The new 'battle of methods.'" *Challenge* 33(1): 33–38.

Thacker, E. (2004). "Foreword: Protocol is as protocol does." In Galloway, G. (Ed.), *Protocol: How control exists after decentralization* (pp. xi–xxii). Cambridge, MA: MIT Press.

Thelwall, M., K. Buckley et al. (2010). "Sentiment strength detection in short informal text." Retrieved from http://www.scit.wlv.ac.uk/~cm1993/papers/SentiStrengthPreprint.doc

Toffler, A. (1980). *The third wave*. London: Collins.

Tolbert, C. J., and R. S. McNeal. (2003). "Unraveling the effects of the Internet on political participation?" *Political Research Quarterly* 56(2): 175–185.

Tulloch, J. (1995). "'We're only a speck in the ocean': The fans as powerless elite." In Jenkins, H., and J. Tulloch (Eds.), *Science fiction audiences: Watching Doctor Who and Star Trek* (pp. 144–172). London: Routledge.

Vaidhyanathan, S. (2004). *The anarchist in the library: How the clash between freedom and control is hacking the real world and crashing the system*. New York: Basic Books.

Van Leeuwen, T. (2005). *Introducing social semiotics*. London: Routledge.

van Looy, J., and J. Baetens. (2003). *Close reading new media: Analyzing electronic literature*. Leuven, Netherlands: Leuven University Press.

Varnelis, K. (Ed.). (2008). *Networked publics*. Cambridge, MA: MIT Press.

Vergeer, M., L. Hermans et al. (2011). "Is the voter only a tweet away? Micro blogging during the 2009 European Parliament election campaign in the Netherlands." *First Monday* 16(8–1).

von Hippel, E. (2005). *Democratizing innovation*. Cambridge, MA: MIT Press.

Wark, M. (2004). *A hacker manifesto*. Cambridge, MA: Harvard University Press.

Warner, M. (2002a). "Publics and counterpublics." *Public Culture* 14(1): 49–90.

———. (2002b). *Publics and counterpublics*. New York: Zone Books.

Wasserman, S., and K. Faust. (1994). *Social network analysis: Methods and applications*. Cambridge, UK: Cambridge University Press.

Watts, D. J. (2003). *Six degrees: The science of a connected age*. New York: Norton.

Weisbrot, D. M. (2008). "Prelude to a school shooting? Assessing threatening behaviors in childhood and adolescence." *Journal of the American Academy of Child & Adolescent Psychiatry* 47: 847–852.

Wellman, B. (1997). "An electronic group is virtually a social network." In Kiesler, S. (Ed.), *Culture of the Internet* (pp. 179–205). Mahwah, NJ: Lawrence Erlbaum.

Wenger, E. (1998). *Communities of practice: Learning, meaning, and identity*. Cambridge, UK: Cambridge University Press.

Wettergren, Å. (2005). *Moving and jamming: Implications for social movement theory*. Karlstad, Sweden: Department of Sociology, Division for Social Sciences, Karlstad University.

White, M. (2010). "Clicktivism is ruining leftist activism." *The Guardian*, 12 August.

Wilbur, W. J., and K. Sirotkin. (1992). "The automatic identification of stop words." *Journal of Information Science* 18(1): 45–55.

Williams, R. (1961). *The long revolution*. London: Chatto & Windus.

Woods, W. A. (1970). "Transition network grammars for natural language analysis." *Communications of the ACM* 13(10): 591–606.

Zipf, G. (1935). *The psycho-biology of language: An introduction to dynamic philology*. Cambridge, MA: MIT Press.

INDEX

ad-hoc publics 51
alienation 16, 89, 90, 91, 95, 104, 139, 148
Anonymous 31, 32, 50
antagonism 3, 16, 47, 56, 60, 120, 143
Arab Spring 49, 51, 140
ARPANET 25, 26

bow-tie model 70

capitalism 2, 3, 5, 7, 12, 15, 16, 17, 32, 135,
    143, 146, 147, 148, 149, 153, 154, 159
CCA 35, 38, 40, 41, 42, 43, 44, 45, 46, 51,
    53, 81, 98, 101, 106, 118, 119
censorship 54, 56, 61, 135
clicktivism 14, 50
collective intelligence 7, 11, 12, 14, 79, 89,
    91, 136
co-occurrence analysis 43, 44, 45, 53, 81,
    102
control 3, 6, 13, 24, 26, 27, 29, 33, 45, 60, 76,
    78, 113, 115, 116, 117, 124, 134, 140,
    141, 143
convergence 5, 63, 156

coping strategies 123
copyright 21, 79, 126, 127, 132, 135
cosmopedia 11, 14, 20, 144
counter-power 2, 17, 18, 66, 140, 149
counterpublic 3, 4, 21, 29, 47, 78, 140, 144
crowdsourcing 15

democracy 13, 14, 15, 17, 18, 21, 50, 54, 57,
    78, 136, 144
disinhibition 78, 95, 96, 107, 123
disruption 2, 7, 18, 21, 22, 23, 27, 29, 30, 34,
    45, 46, 47, 50, 65, 75, 78, 89, 93, 96,
    107, 111, 123, 125, 139, 140, 141, 142,
    143, 145, 146, 147, 148, 149
disruptive spaces 1, 2, 3, 4, 10, 13, 14, 16, 17,
    19, 20, 21, 27, 31, 35, 37, 38, 46, 47, 50,
    60, 78, 79, 80, 93, 124, 126, 140, 141,
    142, 143, 144, 145, 149
distant reading 36
doxa 10, 31, 32, 33, 57

emancipatory use of media 5, 6, 143
exploitation 2, 4, 13, 17, 130

Facebook 15, 68, 77
fan culture 1, 2, 3, 10, 14, 31, 32, 46, 83, 107, 149

Google 113, 114, 115, 116, 117, 139
Graphviz 44

habitus 32, 35, 146
hacking 81, 131, 132, 135, 137
hacktivism 2, 31, 45, 49, 50, 52, 56, 59, 60, 61, 63, 75, 77, 79, 126, 140
hashtags 45, 51, 52, 58, 61, 62, 63, 65, 66, 67, 69, 72, 73, 75, 76, 140
hegemony 1, 2, 4, 5, 7, 19, 20, 21, 22, 23, 29, 32, 34, 45, 46, 47, 76, 124, 143, 144, 145, 146, 148, 151, 157
heterodoxy 30, 32, 33
hive mind 11, 20, 47
hybridity 81, 93, 148, 149, 150

ideology 2, 14, 22, 23, 46, 75, 121, 124, 125, 126, 127, 131, 134, 136, 140, 141, 142

long tail 3, 7, 42, 50, 58, 78, 140, 149

occupy 31, 33, 50, 62, 155, 159
orthodoxy 32, 33

participatory culture 2, 3, 11, 12, 14, 16, 17, 18, 20, 21, 35, 46, 51, 78, 79, 89, 95, 108, 124, 132, 138, 144
peer-to-peer 81, 83, 109, 135
piracy 1, 3, 19, 21, 47, 79, 125, 126, 127, 128, 129, 130, 131, 132, 133, 134, 135, 136, 137, 138, 140
prosumerism 12, 13, 16, 17, 20
protocol 21, 24, 25, 26, 27, 28, 29, 30, 32, 34, 62, 144, 145, 146

remix 1, 2, 21, 31, 32

repressive use of media 5, 6
resistance 1, 4, 13, 19, 20, 29, 32, 34, 46, 47, 62, 63, 131, 142, 145
revolution 55, 68, 70, 76, 77, 94, 154, 157, 158, 159, 160
rhizome 24, 27 15, 143

sentiment analysis 38, 46, 68, 86, 96, 97, 99, 100, 101, 106, 107
slacktivism 1, 14, 50
subactivism 126, 127, 129, 131, 133, 135, 137
subculture 7, 21, 22, 23, 24, 79, 120, 152, 153, 156
subpolitics 47, 125, 126, 129, 130, 133, 137 149, 157
surveillance 56, 57

tactics 4, 5, 16, 19, 28, 47, 77, 133, 140, 135, 149
technopolitics 5, 17, 18
Textometrica 41, 43, 44, 66, 73
triangulation 38, 39, 41, 154, 156
trolls 94, 96, 107
Twitter 1, 15, 39, 46, 49, 51, 52, 53, 54, 56, 57, 60, 61, 62, 63, 66, 68, 69, 70, 71, 72, 76, 77, 78, 139, 140

user-generated content 46, 100, 101, 106, 108, 141, 142

virtual settlements 8, 9, 10, 20, 51, 52, 57, 60
WikiLeaks 45, 51, 52, 53, 54, 55, 56, 57, 58, 60, 61, 62, 63, 140, 151, 157

YouTube 3, 4, 46, 54, 93, 94, 95, 96, 97, 98, 99, 100, 101, 102, 103, 104, 105, 106, 107, 108, 109, 111, 112, 113, 117, 118, 119, 120, 121, 123, 124, 141, 152, 153, 155, 156, 157, 158, 159